The Social Security Clarity Guide

A Step-by-Step Guide to Claiming Strategies, Spousal Benefits, Medicare Timing, and Avoiding Costly Mistakes in Retirement

by

Preston Wade

Table of Contents

A Note Before You Begin

This book is a general educational guide to how Social Security and Medicare work in the United States. It is designed to help you understand the mechanics of the system — how claiming age affects your benefit, how spousal and survivor benefits are calculated, how taxation works, how Medicare enrollment windows function, and how recent legislative changes affect certain public sector workers — so that you can ask better questions and make more informed decisions.

It is not personalized financial, legal, or tax advice, and it should not be treated as a substitute for guidance from the Social Security Administration (SSA), a licensed financial advisor, or a qualified tax professional. Every reader's situation is different, and the right claiming strategy for one household can be the wrong one for another.

You will also notice that this book intentionally avoids presenting exact dollar figures as if they were fixed forever. Social Security benefit formulas, taxable income thresholds, Medicare premiums, and IRMAA brackets are all adjusted periodically — some annually for inflation through cost-of-living adjustments (COLA), others only when Congress changes the law. A number that is accurate this year may be outdated next year. Wherever specific figures matter to your own decisions, verify the current numbers directly at ssa.gov or medicare.gov, or ask a licensed advisor to check them for you.

Nothing in this book guarantees any particular financial outcome. Claiming strategies described here are general patterns that tend to apply to most people in most circumstances — they are starting points for a conversation, not guarantees. Use this book to build your understanding, then take your specific numbers to a professional or to the SSA directly before making an irreversible decision.

With that groundwork laid, let's begin.

Chapter One: How Social Security Actually Works

Most people spend decades paying into Social Security before they spend more than a few minutes trying to understand how it actually works. That is not a criticism — the system is confusing by design, built up over nearly a century of legislation, formula adjustments, and add-on programs. But the decisions you make about when and how to claim your benefit are among the most consequential financial decisions of your retirement, and they are very difficult to reverse once made. This chapter lays the foundation everything else in this book builds on.

The Basic Idea

Social Security is, at its core, a social insurance program. While you work, you and your employer each pay a payroll tax (self-employed workers pay both halves) into the system. In exchange, once you meet certain eligibility requirements, you become entitled to a monthly benefit in retirement, and your family may become entitled to benefits connected to your work record — spousal benefits, survivor benefits, and in some cases benefits for dependent children.

It helps to think of Social Security less like a personal savings account and more like a pension that the government administers on behalf of the whole working population. The money you contribute today is used to pay benefits to people who are currently retired; when you retire, the workers of that era will be funding your benefit. This "pay-as-you-go" structure is one of the most misunderstood aspects of the program, and it explains why the system's finances are periodically debated in the news — but it does not change how your individual benefit is calculated, which is what this book focuses on.

Earning Your Eligibility

To qualify for retirement benefits, you generally need to accumulate 40 "credits" over your working life. In a given year, you earn up to four credits, so most people become fully insured after about ten years of work — though the specific amount of earnings required to receive a credit changes each year with wage growth, so if you are close to that threshold, it is worth checking your current earnings record on your "my Social Security" account at ssa.gov.

It is worth noting that these ten years do not need to be consecutive, and they do not need to be your most recent years of work. If you worked steadily in your twenties and thirties, then stepped away from paid work for an extended period — to raise children, care for a family member, or pursue other work that did not pay into the system — those earlier years still count toward your 40 credits, as long as you meet the total.

How Your Benefit Amount Is Calculated

This is the part most people skip past, and it is exactly the part worth understanding, because it explains almost everything else in this book.

The Social Security Administration looks at your entire earnings history, indexes your earnings for wage growth (so that money you earned decades ago is adjusted to reflect today's wage levels, rather than being compared dollar-for-dollar), and then takes your highest 35 years of indexed earnings. It averages those 35 years to produce a figure called your Average Indexed Monthly Earnings, or AIME.

That AIME is then run through a formula — called the Primary Insurance Amount, or PIA, formula — that is deliberately progressive. It applies a higher percentage to your first slice of average earnings, a smaller percentage to the next slice, and an even smaller percentage to earnings above that. The practical effect is that Social Security replaces a larger share of income for lower earners than for higher earners. This is one of the built-in design features of the program: it is meant to provide a stronger floor of protection for people who earned less over their working lives, while still rewarding higher earners with a larger dollar benefit overall.

Your PIA is the benefit you would receive if you claimed exactly at your Full Retirement Age (FRA), which we will cover in detail in the next chapter. Every other claiming age either reduces or increases that number.

The Thirty-Five-Year Rule Matters More Than People Realize

Because the formula uses your highest 35 years, working an extra year — or even a partial year — late in your career can meaningfully raise your benefit, but only if that year's earnings are higher than one of the 35 years currently being counted. If you already have 35 solid years of earnings and your income has dropped in recent years (a common pattern for people who reduce hours before retiring), continuing to work in that lower-earning period will not increase your benefit and may not be worth optimizing around from a Social Security perspective alone.

On the other hand, if you have fewer than 35 years of covered earnings — common for people who spent significant time out of the paid workforce, or who spent years working in jobs not covered by Social Security — the missing years are counted as zeros in the average. Filling in even a few of those zero years with real earnings, even modest ones, can raise your average and therefore your benefit meaningfully. This is one of the more overlooked planning opportunities: a few additional years of part-time work in your late fifties or early sixties, purely to replace zero-earning years in the formula, can have an outsized effect on your eventual benefit.

Consider a hypothetical retiree — we'll call her Diane — who worked steadily from her early twenties through her late forties, then stepped back from paid work for eight years while caring for aging parents, before returning to part-time work in her late fifties. Those eight zero-earning years were dragging her average down. When she returned to part-time work, even at a modest salary, each of those working years replaced a zero in her 35-year average, raising her eventual benefit by a noticeable amount. She did not need to work full-time or for many more years — she needed her working years to outnumber her zero years in the specific 35-year window the formula uses.

What "Full Retirement Age" Really Means

Full Retirement Age is not a single fixed number — it depends on the year you were born, and it has been gradually rising. For people born in the 1940s and early 1950s, FRA was 66. For people born from the mid-1950s through 1959, FRA rises gradually, generally by two months per birth year. For anyone born in 1960 or later, FRA is 67.

This matters because FRA is the anchor point for every claiming calculation in this book. Claim before your FRA, and your monthly benefit is permanently reduced. Claim after your FRA (up to age 70), and your monthly benefit is permanently increased through delayed retirement credits. We will walk through exactly how those adjustments work in the next two chapters — but for now, the important habit to build is this: whenever you think about "your benefit," ask yourself which age you're really talking about. A benefit estimate is meaningless without a claiming age attached to it.

Where to Find Your Real Numbers

Everything in this book describes how the system works in general terms. Your specific benefit estimate — the actual dollar figures for claiming at 62, at your FRA, and at 70 — is available to you directly through your "my Social Security" online account at ssa.gov. This is, without exaggeration, the single most useful document you can pull before making any claiming decision. It reflects your actual earnings history and gives estimates at multiple claiming ages side by side.

If you have not created this account yet, consider it the first homework assignment of this book. Everything that follows will make more sense once you can see your own numbers next to the concepts being discussed.

What Counts as "Covered" Earnings

Not every job in the United States pays into Social Security. Most private-sector employment does, along with most federal civilian employment hired in recent decades and the majority of state and local government jobs. But a meaningful minority of state and local government positions — certain teaching jobs, some police and fire departments, and other public roles depending on the state — operate under their own separate pension systems instead of, or in addition to, Social Security. Railroad employment has its own entirely separate retirement system as well, administered by the Railroad Retirement Board rather than the SSA, with its own rules that mirror but don't exactly match Social Security's.

This distinction matters because your 35-year earnings average, described above, is built only from years in which you had covered earnings — years worked in a non-covered job simply don't contribute to the calculation at all, positively or negatively, unless they also happened to include some Social Security-covered income. We'll return to this topic in much more depth in Chapter Ten, which is devoted specifically to how non-covered government work has historically interacted with Social Security, and what changed with the Social Security Fairness Act. For now, the important thing to recognize is simply that "how many years have I worked" and "how many years count toward my Social Security benefit" are not always the same question, and if any part of your career involved a job that didn't withhold Social Security payroll taxes, it's worth understanding which years those were before you start estimating your own benefit.

How Cost-of-Living Adjustments Work Once You're Receiving Benefits

Everything described so far in this chapter explains how your benefit is calculated at the point you claim it. But Social Security benefits don't stay frozen at that starting dollar amount for the rest of your life. Once you're receiving benefits, they are generally adjusted annually through a cost-of-living adjustment, or COLA, tied to a measure of inflation. In years with meaningful inflation, COLA increases can be substantial; in years with very low inflation, the increase may be small or, in rare cases, zero.

This is a genuinely valuable feature of the program, and one that sets it apart from many private pensions and annuities, which often pay a fixed dollar amount for life with no automatic inflation adjustment at all. Over a retirement that might last twenty, thirty, or more years, inflation protection compounds in importance — a fixed-dollar income that felt comfortable at the start of retirement can feel quite different two or three decades later without some mechanism to keep pace with rising prices. COLA doesn't guarantee your purchasing power will never erode at all (the specific inflation measure used doesn't perfectly track every retiree's actual spending patterns, particularly healthcare costs, which often rise faster than general inflation), but it does mean your benefit is not simply left behind by inflation the way a purely fixed payment would be.

It's worth noting that COLA applies to your benefit however you claimed it — whether you claimed at 62, at FRA, or at 70, once you're receiving a benefit, that dollar amount receives the same annual adjustment as anyone else's. COLA is not a reason to claim earlier or later in itself; it's simply a feature that applies uniformly once you're in the system.

Common Misconceptions About the Benefit Formula

A few misunderstandings about how benefits are calculated come up often enough to be worth addressing directly, since clearing them up now will make the rest of this book easier to follow.

The first is the belief that Social Security functions like a personal account where your specific contributions are set aside and later returned to you, similar to a 401(k). As described earlier in this chapter, that's not how the program works — your benefit is calculated using a formula based on your earnings history, but the payroll taxes you contributed over your career were used to pay benefits to retirees at the time you were working, not saved in an account with your name on it. This doesn't affect your right to a benefit calculated under the formula, but it does mean thinking of your "contributions" as a running balance you're simply withdrawing from is not an accurate model of how the system operates.

The second misconception is that working longer always increases your benefit. As explained above, additional years of work only raise your benefit if they replace one of the lower-earning years currently counted in your highest-35-years average. If you already have 35 strong earning years, additional years of work beyond that point may still make sense for other financial reasons — continued income, employer health coverage, personal fulfillment — but they will not, by themselves, increase your Social Security benefit unless the new year's earnings are higher than the lowest year currently being counted.

The third misconception is that your benefit is based on your final salary or your peak earning year alone, similar to how some traditional pensions are calculated. Social

Security uses a 35-year average, not a peak-year or final-year calculation, which is one of the reasons a full career of steady, moderate earnings can sometimes produce a similar or even higher benefit than a shorter career with a few very high-earning years, depending on the specific numbers involved.

Reviewing Your Earnings Record for Errors

Because your entire benefit calculation depends on your recorded earnings history, it's worth periodically reviewing that record for accuracy — errors do happen, whether from an employer misreporting earnings, a name or Social Security number mismatch, or simple administrative mistakes accumulated over a long working life. Your "my Social Security" account displays your full year-by-year earnings history as recorded by the SSA, and comparing it against your own records (old tax returns or W-2 forms, for instance) is a worthwhile exercise, particularly if you've changed your name, changed jobs frequently, or worked for smaller employers where administrative errors may be more likely.

If you do find a discrepancy, the SSA has a process for correcting earnings records, though it generally works best with documentation from the years in question, so don't wait until you're about to claim benefits to check — the earlier a potential error is caught, the easier it typically is to gather the supporting documentation needed to correct it.

Self-Employment and Social Security

If you've spent any part of your career self-employed, it's worth understanding how that work fits into everything described in this chapter. Self-employed individuals generally pay both the employee and employer portions of Social Security payroll tax, often referred to as self-employment tax, through their annual tax filing rather than through payroll withholding. This means self-employment income, when reported and taxed properly, counts as covered earnings toward your 40 credits and toward your 35-year average in essentially the same way as employee wages do.

A common pitfall worth flagging: some self-employed individuals, particularly those running very small or informal businesses, are tempted to underreport income to reduce their current tax bill. Beyond the general legal risks of doing so, it's worth understanding the Social Security-specific cost: underreported self-employment income means a lower recorded earnings history, which can translate directly into a smaller future Social Security benefit. Accurately reporting self-employment income isn't just a matter of tax compliance — it's also, in effect, an investment in your own future benefit calculation.

A Brief Note on Disability Benefits and the Transition to Retirement

This book focuses primarily on retirement benefits, but it's worth briefly distinguishing them from Social Security Disability Insurance

(SSDI), since the two programs are related but distinct, and some readers may be receiving or considering one while thinking about the other. SSDI provides benefits to people who become unable to work due to a qualifying disability before reaching retirement age, based on their own earnings record and work credits, following a different, disability-specific application and evaluation process than retirement benefits.

If you are receiving SSDI when you reach your Full Retirement Age, your disability benefit generally converts automatically to a retirement benefit at that point, generally at the same dollar amount, without requiring a new application — the underlying calculation is designed to treat this as a continuation rather than a new claim. This is a helpful, often under-recognized feature of the system: people receiving SSDI don't need to separately navigate the claiming-age decisions described throughout this book, since their transition to retirement benefits at FRA happens automatically. If you have questions about your own SSDI-to-retirement transition, the SSA can confirm the specifics of your case directly.

A Short History, for Context

Social Security was established in 1935, during the Great Depression, initially as a more limited program than the one that exists today. Over the following decades, it was expanded significantly — spousal benefits, survivor benefits, disability benefits, and automatic cost-of-living adjustments were all added at different points, generally through legislation responding to identified gaps or changing social and economic conditions. The Social Security Fairness Act, covered in Chapter Ten, is simply the most recent example of a pattern that has repeated throughout the program's history: adjustments made as policymakers identify ways the existing rules don't serve certain groups of workers and families well.

Understanding this history isn't necessary to make good decisions about your own benefits, but it may be reassuring context: the specific rules described in this book are not ancient or immovable — they are the current state of a program that has evolved substantially over nine decades and continues to be periodically refined. This is also, again, precisely why this book repeatedly emphasizes checking current figures and rules at ssa.gov rather than treating any specific number as permanent.

Dependent Benefits for Children of Retired or Disabled Workers

While this book focuses primarily on the retirement-age decisions most readers are navigating, it's worth briefly noting that dependent children of a retired or disabled worker can, in some circumstances, be eligible for a benefit based on that worker's record — generally applying to unmarried children under 18 (or under 19 if still a full-time student in secondary school), or to an adult child whose qualifying disability began before age 22. This is most relevant to readers who became parents later in life, or who are raising grandchildren or other dependents, and find themselves approaching their own retirement claiming decision with a dependent child still in the picture. If this applies to your household, it's worth raising directly with the SSA when you apply for your own retirement benefit, since it can add a meaningful dimension to your household's total benefit that a purely individual claiming analysis would miss entirely.

The Family Maximum

Related to the point above, when multiple family members are eligible for benefits based on a single worker's record — for instance, a retired worker, a spouse receiving a spousal benefit, and a dependent child all drawing from the same record simultaneously — Social Security applies a limit called the family maximum, which caps the total amount payable to a family based on one worker's earnings record. When the combined total of individual benefit amounts would exceed this cap, the individual benefits (other than the worker's own retirement benefit, which is generally not reduced by this provision) are generally reduced proportionately to bring the family total within the cap. This is a fairly specialized provision that mainly affects households with multiple simultaneous dependent or spousal claims on a single record, but it's worth being aware that it exists if your household situation involves several people drawing on the same worker's earnings history at once — the SSA can walk you through exactly how it applies to your specific family composition.

Putting Chapter One in Context for the Rest of This Book

Everything in the chapters that follow builds on the concepts introduced here: the Primary Insurance Amount as the anchor figure for every claiming-age adjustment in Chapter Two, the 35-year average as the foundation spousal and survivor benefits ultimately trace back to in Chapters Four and Five, and covered versus non-covered earnings as the dividing line that Chapter Ten's discussion of the Social Security Fairness Act depends on entirely. If any part of this chapter felt dense on a first read, it may be worth returning to it again after finishing the rest of the book, since the later chapters tend to make the earlier mechanics click into place through concrete application rather than abstract description. Understanding your PIA, your 35-year average, and your covered earnings history is, in a real sense, the vocabulary the rest of this book is written in.

A Quick Reference for the Terms Introduced in This Chapter

Because this chapter introduced several terms that recur throughout the rest of the book, it may help to have them summarized in one place. AIME, or Average Indexed Monthly Earnings, is your career average based on your highest 35 years of wage-indexed earnings. PIA, or Primary Insurance Amount, is the benefit produced by running your AIME through Social Security's progressive formula — the amount you'd receive if you claimed exactly at your Full Retirement Age. FRA, or

Full Retirement Age, is the birth-year-dependent age (66 to 67) at which you receive your full PIA with no reduction or bonus. Covered earnings are wages or self-employment income on which Social Security payroll taxes were paid, as distinct from non-covered earnings from certain government positions. Keeping these four terms clear as you move through the rest of the book will make each subsequent chapter's discussion of claiming ages, spousal percentages, and benefit calculations considerably easier to follow.

Key Takeaways

Social Security is a social insurance program funded by payroll taxes, not a personal savings account, though your own earnings history directly determines your benefit amount.

Eligibility generally requires 40 work credits, roughly ten years of covered work, which do not need to be consecutive or recent.

Your benefit is based on your highest 35 years of indexed earnings, run through a progressive formula that replaces a larger share of income for lower earners.

Full Retirement Age depends on your birth year — 66 for those born earlier, gradually rising to 67 for those born in 1960 or later — and it is the anchor point for every claiming-age adjustment.

Create your "my Social Security" account at ssa.gov early. It gives you your real, personalized numbers, which is far more useful than any general estimate.

Chapter Two: When to Claim: 62 vs. Full Retirement Age vs. 70

If there is one decision this book exists to help you think through carefully, it is this one. You can begin claiming retirement benefits as early as age 62, and you can delay all the way to age 70 — a full eight-year window, during which your monthly benefit amount can swing dramatically depending on when you start. Unlike many financial decisions, this one is largely irreversible once made (with narrow exceptions we'll cover), which is exactly why it deserves careful thought rather than a snap decision made the week you leave your job.

The Three Reference Points

Age 62 is the earliest age at which most people can claim retirement benefits. Claiming here locks in a permanently reduced monthly benefit — reduced because you are, in effect, choosing to receive a smaller amount over what is likely to be a longer number of total years.

Full Retirement Age (FRA) — 66 to 67 depending on your birth year, as covered in the previous chapter — is where you receive exactly 100% of your calculated Primary Insurance Amount, with no reduction and no bonus.

Age 70 is the latest age at which it makes sense to delay claiming retirement benefits, because delayed retirement credits stop accruing at 70. Waiting past 70 provides no further increase to your retirement benefit, so there is no financial reason to delay beyond that point.

How the Reduction for Early Claiming Works

Claiming before FRA reduces your benefit based on how many months early you claim. The reduction is not linear across the whole range — it is steeper for the 36 months immediately before FRA, and shallower for any months earlier than that. In practical terms, someone claiming a full 60 months early (for someone with an FRA of 67, that means claiming at 62) typically ends up with a monthly benefit reduced by somewhere in the neighborhood of 25 to 30 percent compared to their FRA amount, depending on their specific FRA. Someone whose FRA is 66 and who claims at 62 (48 months early) will see a somewhat smaller percentage reduction than someone whose FRA is 67 claiming at that same age 62, because they are claiming fewer months ahead of their own FRA.

This is one of the most important things to understand about the "claim at 62" decision: because FRA itself has shifted for younger generations, the exact percentage reduction for claiming at 62 is not the same for everyone. Your personalized estimate at ssa.gov will show you the precise figure for your birth year.

How Delayed Retirement Credits Work

The reverse is true for delaying past FRA. For every year you wait beyond FRA, up to age 70, your benefit increases by a fixed percentage — commonly referenced as roughly 8% per year for people reaching FRA in recent years, applied on a monthly basis rather than all at once on your birthday. So someone with an FRA of 67 who waits until 70 — three additional years — could see their benefit roughly 24% higher than their FRA amount, again subject to the exact current formula, which you should confirm through your own ssa.gov estimate.

Put the two effects together, and the total spread between claiming at 62 and claiming at 70 is substantial — often in the range of 70 to 80 percent difference in monthly benefit amount between the earliest and latest claiming ages, depending on your specific FRA. That is not a rounding error. It is the difference between a comfortable monthly income floor and a tight one, sustained for the rest of your life.

Why It Isn't Simply "Wait as Long as Possible"

Given numbers like that, it's tempting to conclude that everyone should simply wait until 70. But the math is built around life expectancy assumptions, and Social Security's delayed credits are, broadly speaking, designed to be roughly actuarially neutral for someone who lives an average lifespan — meaning that if you live to a statistically average age, the total lifetime benefits you receive should come out similar whether you claim early and receive smaller checks for longer, or claim late and receive larger checks for a shorter period. The "right" answer changes dramatically based on factors specific to you:

Health and family longevity. If you have reason to expect a shorter-than-average lifespan — based on your own health history or your family's — claiming earlier may allow you to receive more total value from the program, even though your monthly check is smaller.

Immediate income need. If you have no other source of income and leaving the workforce at 62 without claiming would mean going without income, the theoretical benefits of waiting may not be practical for your household.

Marital status and spousal considerations. As we'll cover in the next two chapters, your claiming decision can affect not just your own benefit, but your spouse's spousal benefit while you're both alive, and your spouse's survivor benefit after you're gone. This is often the single biggest factor that gets overlooked in a "just look at my own numbers" approach.

Other income and taxes. Claiming while still working can trigger the retirement earnings test (which we'll explain below), and it can also push more of your benefit into taxable territory, which we cover in Chapter Seven.

Break-even analysis limitations. It's common to see "break-even age" calculators that tell you the age at which delaying pays off compared to claiming early. These can be a useful reference point, but they generally assume you invest nothing, treat every dollar the same regardless of when you receive it, and don't account for taxes, health changes, or the value of guaranteed income later in life when you may be less able to manage investments. Treat break-even calculations as one data point, not the whole answer.

The Retirement Earnings Test

If you claim benefits before your FRA and continue working, a rule called the retirement earnings test may temporarily withhold part of your benefit if your earnings exceed a certain annual limit — a limit that is adjusted periodically and should be checked at ssa.gov for the current year. Importantly, this is not money you lose forever: any amount withheld under the earnings test is later factored back into your benefit calculation once you reach FRA, effectively raising your monthly benefit going forward to account for the months withheld. Many people find this rule counterintuitive and assume they are permanently losing benefits by working while claiming early — that is generally not the case, though the cash-flow timing can still matter to your household budget.

Once you reach FRA, the earnings test no longer applies at all — you can earn any amount from work while receiving your full benefit with no withholding.

Consider a Hypothetical Household

Picture a retiree we'll call Marcus, age 61, planning to leave a physically demanding job. Marcus has some savings but not enough to comfortably self-fund three to eight years without any income. For Marcus, claiming close to 62 may be the realistic choice, even knowing the monthly benefit will be permanently smaller, because the alternative — depleting savings rapidly or returning to physically difficult work — carries its own real costs.

Now picture a second hypothetical retiree, Renata, age 64, still working in a role she doesn't mind continuing, with a pension and investment accounts that can comfortably cover her expenses for several more years. For Renata, delaying to 70 may make far more sense: she doesn't need the income immediately, she's in good health with a family history of longevity, and the larger, delayed benefit functions as a form of longevity insurance — protecting her against the risk of living a very long life and running short of other resources late in retirement.

Neither choice is "correct" in the abstract. Both are reasonable responses to different circumstances. The goal of this chapter is not to tell you which age to pick, but to make sure you understand the mechanics well enough to evaluate your own circumstances clearly — ideally with your actual ssa.gov estimates in front of you, and ideally in conversation with a financial advisor who can see your full financial picture.

Can You Change Your Mind After Claiming?

There are two narrow paths for reversing an early claiming decision, and it's worth knowing they exist even though neither is a general "undo" button.

First, within 12 months of first claiming, you can withdraw your application entirely, but you must repay all benefits received to that point, and this option can only be used once in your lifetime.

Second, once you reach FRA, you can voluntarily suspend your benefit (even if you claimed it before FRA) up until age 70, which stops payments but allows delayed retirement credits to begin accruing again from that point forward. This second option can be a useful tool for someone who claimed early out of necessity but later found their financial situation improved.

Both of these mechanisms have specific rules and current-year details that should be verified directly with the SSA before relying on them.

A Closer Look at How the Reduction and Credit Schedules Actually Work

It's worth walking through the mechanics of the reduction and credit schedules in a bit more detail, because the fact that the early-claiming reduction isn't a single flat percentage across the whole 62-to-FRA range surprises many people.

For the 36 months immediately preceding your FRA, each month of early claiming reduces your benefit by a certain fraction of a percent — roughly five-ninths of one percent per month, under rules that have applied for some time, though as always, confirm the current figure. For any additional months earlier than that 36-month window (relevant mainly to people whose FRA is 67, since claiming at 62 for them means up to 60 months early), the reduction rate for those additional early months is somewhat smaller per month than the rate for the 36 months closest to FRA. The practical effect is that the "cost" of each additional month of early claiming isn't perfectly uniform — the months furthest from FRA are individually slightly less costly, per month, than the months closest to FRA, though the cumulative effect across the full 62-to-67 range still adds up to a substantial total reduction.

Delayed retirement credits, by contrast, do accrue at a steady, uniform monthly rate from FRA up to age 70 — commonly cited as two-thirds of one percent per month, which compounds to roughly 8% for a full year of delay, for people reaching FRA in recent years (this rate has changed over past decades and could be confirmed for your specific birth year). Because this rate is uniform, there's no "sweet spot" month between FRA and 70 where delaying suddenly becomes more or less valuable per month than any other month in that range — each additional month of delay adds roughly the same proportional increase.

The Break-Even Age Concept, Used Correctly

Break-even analysis is one of the most commonly referenced tools in Social Security claiming discussions, and it's worth understanding both what it tells you and where its limitations lie, since it's frequently presented as more definitive than it really is.

At its simplest, a break-even calculation compares two claiming ages — say, 62 and 70 — and asks: at what age would the total cumulative benefits received under the later claiming age catch up to and surpass the total cumulative benefits received under the earlier claiming age, given that the earlier claim started collecting sooner but at a smaller monthly amount? For a comparison between 62 and 70, this break-even age commonly falls somewhere in the early-to-mid eighties, though the exact age depends on your specific FRA and the current reduction and credit percentages.

The limitation is that a simple break-even calculation typically assumes the money isn't invested, ignores taxes, ignores the insurance value of a larger guaranteed payment late in life (discussed in Chapter Three), and treats every year of life as equally likely, when in reality your own health and family history might reasonably shift your personal expectation above or below population averages. A break-even age is a useful reference point — it tells you roughly how long you'd need to live for the "wait" strategy to produce more total dollars in a simplified comparison — but it shouldn't be treated as the single deciding factor, particularly for a married couple where the survivor benefit implications (Chapter Five) often matter more than the break-even math for either individual spouse alone.

Common Claiming Mistakes Worth Avoiding

A few patterns show up repeatedly among people who later say they regret their claiming decision, and naming them directly may help you avoid the same experience.

Claiming immediately at 62 out of habit or a vague sense that "sooner is safer," without actually running the numbers or considering household implications, is one of the most common. For some households, 62 genuinely is the right answer, as discussed earlier in this chapter — but it should be a considered decision, not a default one.

A second common mistake is the reverse: assuming that delaying to 70 is always optimal without weighing the practical reality of the household's income needs during the delay years, sometimes leading people to draw down savings faster than intended, or take on unwanted part-time work, simply to "hold out" for the larger benefit.

A third mistake, specific to couples, is each spouse optimizing their own claiming age independently, without considering how the two decisions interact — particularly the survivor benefit implications of the higher earner's choice, covered in depth in Chapter Five. Because so much of the value in this decision comes from the household perspective, treating it as two separate individual decisions is a common way meaningful value gets left unclaimed.

A fourth mistake is failing to account for Medicare timing (Chapter Eight) as a separate decision from the Social Security claiming decision — people sometimes assume the two are linked, delay both together, and inadvertently trigger a Medicare late enrollment penalty that has nothing to do with their Social Security claiming strategy at all.

The Value of Bringing a Professional Into This Specific Decision

Because the claiming-age decision is largely irreversible, involves genuinely complex trade-offs, and often carries significant lifetime financial weight, it's one of the areas of retirement planning where the cost of professional guidance is frequently justified by the value of getting the decision right. A financial advisor familiar with Social Security claiming strategy can model out your specific numbers across different claiming ages, account for your other income sources and tax situation, and help you see interactions (like the survivor-benefit implications covered in Chapter Five) that are easy to miss when looking at your own numbers in isolation.

If you don't already work with a financial advisor, some organizations and financial professionals offer Social Security-specific claiming analysis as a standalone service, separate from broader investment management, which may be a reasonable middle ground if you're not looking for ongoing portfolio management but do want expert eyes on this specific decision. As with any financial service, it's worth understanding how the advisor is compensated and confirming they don't have a conflict of interest that might bias their recommendation toward a particular claiming age.

A Brief Note on Citizenship and Residency Considerations

Most of this book assumes a U.S. citizen or long-term resident with a standard domestic work history, since that describes the majority of readers. If your situation involves significant time living or working outside the United States, non-citizen status, or a mixed work history across countries, be aware that additional rules can apply — including, in some cases, international Social Security agreements (sometimes called "totalization agreements") between the U.S. and certain other countries, which can affect how work credits from each country count toward eligibility in either system. These situations involve enough specific variation that general guidance in a book like this one isn't sufficient — if this describes your situation, a direct conversation with the SSA, ideally supplemented by a professional familiar with international Social Security agreements, is the right next step rather than trying to apply the general domestic rules described throughout this book to a more complex cross-border history.

Reconsidering the Decision If Your Circumstances Change Before You File

Because the claiming-age decision covered in this chapter is something many people think about for months or years before actually filing, it's worth remembering that your plan doesn't need to be locked in early — you can continue to revisit and adjust your intended claiming age right up until you actually submit an application, based on changes in your health, your household's financial situation, or new information you learn along the way. Thinking of your claiming-age plan as a working hypothesis that you refine as circumstances evolve, rather than a firm decision made once and never revisited until the day you file, tends to produce better outcomes than committing early and mentally closing the door on reconsidering.

Special Circumstances: Claiming While Managing a Chronic Health Condition

If you're managing a chronic health condition that isn't severe enough to qualify for disability benefits but that reasonably affects your expectations about your own longevity or your capacity to continue working, it's worth folding that consideration explicitly into your claiming-age analysis rather than setting it aside. This doesn't mean a chronic condition automatically points toward claiming early — some chronic conditions are well managed and compatible with a long life, while others carry a more meaningful effect on life expectancy — but it does mean this is exactly the kind of personal factor that should weigh more heavily in your own decision than any generic average-lifespan assumption. A conversation with your own physician about general life-expectancy considerations tied to your specific health situation, while inherently uncertain, can be a more useful input than a population-wide statistic that doesn't reflect your individual circumstances.

A Note on Part-Time or Phased Retirement

An increasing number of people approach retirement gradually rather than stopping work abruptly on a single date — reducing hours, consulting part-time, or taking on lighter seasonal work for a period before fully retiring. This phased approach interacts with several concepts covered in this chapter and the next. If you claim Social Security before your FRA while still working part-time, remember the retirement earnings test from earlier in this chapter, which may temporarily withhold benefits if your part-time earnings exceed the annual limit — though, as covered above, withheld amounts are generally credited back into your benefit at FRA rather than lost outright. If your phased retirement involves meaningfully reduced income compared to your peak earning years, it's also worth checking whether those final working years are affecting your 35-year average from Chapter One in a way worth being aware of, and revisiting Chapter Nine's IRMAA planning guidance if your income is stepping down gradually rather than dropping all at once, since a multi-year income transition affects the two-year IRMAA lookback differently than an abrupt retirement does.

Documenting Your Decision for Your Own Future Reference

Once you've worked through the claiming-age concepts in this chapter and reached a tentative decision, it's worth writing down not just the age you're leaning toward, but the reasoning behind it — your health considerations, your other income sources, your household discussion if applicable, and the specific ssa.gov estimates you were working from at the time. Circumstances change, and rules occasionally change too, but having a written record of your original reasoning makes it much easier to evaluate, a year or two later, whether that reasoning still holds or whether something material has shifted enough to warrant reconsidering. This simple habit —

treating your claiming plan as a documented decision rather than a vague intention held only in memory — tends to lead to more consistent, confident follow-through when the actual filing date arrives.

What to Do if You're Approaching 62 and Feel Undecided

If you're nearing 62 and still genuinely unsure which claiming age fits your circumstances, it's worth remembering that you are not required to decide right at that milestone. Reaching 62 opens the window to claim — it doesn't close any other window except the earliest possible starting point. If you're uncertain, a reasonable default is to continue gathering information (your ssa.gov estimates, a conversation with a financial advisor, the household discussion described later in this book) rather than claiming reflexively simply because the option has become available. Indecision at 62 is not itself a problem; claiming out of a vague sense of obligation to "use" the benefit as soon as it's available, without having actually worked through the considerations in this chapter, is the pattern more worth avoiding.

Key Takeaways

Claiming ranges from age 62 to age 70, with your benefit permanently reduced for early claiming and permanently increased for delayed claiming through delayed retirement credits, which stop accruing at 70.

The difference between claiming at 62 and 70 is substantial — often 70 to 80 percent in monthly benefit amount — but the "right" age depends heavily on your health, other income, marital situation, and tax picture, not on the dollar spread alone.

The retirement earnings test can temporarily withhold benefits if you claim early and keep working above an annual limit, but the withheld amount is generally credited back into your benefit at FRA — it is not simply lost.

Two narrow mechanisms — a 12-month withdrawal window and a post-FRA voluntary suspension — allow limited course correction after claiming, but neither is a general do-over.

Chapter Three: The Real Cost of Claiming Early (and the Real Reward of Waiting)

The previous chapter walked through the mechanics of the claiming-age decision. This chapter goes deeper into a question people often ask but rarely have framed clearly for them: what are you actually trading away when you claim early, and what are you actually buying when you wait?

Reframing the Question

It's natural to think of "claiming early" as losing money and "waiting" as gaining money. But that framing misses what's really happening. You aren't losing or gaining money in some abstract sense — you're choosing between two different income streams: a smaller check that starts sooner and continues for more years, or a larger check that starts later and continues for fewer years (from that later starting point onward). Total lifetime benefits paid can end up similar under either path if you live an average lifespan, because the delayed credit and early reduction formulas were built with that rough balance in mind.

What changes based on your choice is not so much the total dollars over an "average" lifetime, but the shape of your income and the risks you are protected against or exposed to.

The Insurance Framing

One of the most useful ways to think about delaying Social Security is not as an investment decision but as an insurance decision. Insurance, in general, is something you buy to protect against a risk you can't predict for yourself individually — you don't know in advance if your house will burn down, but you know that as a group, some houses will, so you pay a premium to protect against that specific outcome for your own household.

Longevity is similar. None of us knows our own lifespan in advance. Some people will live shorter-than-average lives; others will live well past typical life expectancy, some into their nineties or beyond. The financial risk of a long life is that you outlive your other savings and are left, in your eighties or nineties, dependent primarily on a fixed income that may not be enough.

A larger, delayed Social Security benefit is one of the few tools available that directly protects against that specific risk. Unlike most investments, it is guaranteed for life, adjusted annually for inflation through the cost-of-living adjustment, and cannot be outlived or run out. Viewed this way, delaying claiming is less "gambling that I'll live a long time" and more "buying protection in case I do."

What You Give Up by Delaying

Of course, delaying isn't free. The most obvious cost is the years of smaller (or zero) benefit payments while you wait — years during which you may need to draw down other savings, continue working, or rely on a spouse's income instead. For some households, this simply isn't feasible, and that's a legitimate, practical constraint, not a mistake.

There's also a mortality risk in the opposite direction: if you delay and then pass away relatively soon after claiming, or before claiming at all, you will have received less in total lifetime benefits than if you had claimed earlier. This is uncomfortable to think about, but it's part of why claiming decisions are so personal — they depend in part on things nobody can know for certain in advance.

Consider a Side-by-Side Illustration

To make this concrete without relying on dollar figures that will be outdated by the time you read this, consider two hypothetical versions of the same retiree, whom we'll call Theo, with an FRA of 67.

Version one: Theo claims at 62. He receives a reduced monthly benefit starting five years earlier than his FRA, and it stays at that reduced level (adjusted for inflation) for the rest of his life.

Version two: Theo delays and claims at 70. He receives no retirement benefit for eight years past his earliest eligibility, but from age 70 onward, his monthly benefit is meaningfully higher — again, adjusted for inflation for the rest of his life — than either the age-62 or the FRA amount would have been.

If Theo lives into his mid-eighties or beyond, version two generally produces more total lifetime income, sometimes substantially more, because the higher monthly amount compounds over many years of receipt. If Theo passes away in his early seventies, version one would have produced more total lifetime income, because he received payments for a longer overall period even though each payment was smaller.

Neither version is "wrong" to choose in advance — the point of this illustration isn't to tell you which one Theo should pick, but to show clearly why the decision is genuinely a trade-off, not a decision with one obviously correct answer that applies to everyone.

Beyond Your Own Lifespan: The Household View

For married couples, the calculation gets another layer, because Social Security claiming decisions affect a household, not just an individual — and this is where a purely "my own break-even age" analysis tends to fall short. We'll go into this in detail in the next two chapters, but the short version is this: the benefit of the higher earner in a couple often becomes the survivor benefit for the lower earner after the higher earner passes away. That means a decision to delay claiming isn't just insurance against the higher earner's own longevity — it can also be insurance protecting the household's surviving spouse, who may go on to live many more years as a widow or widower.

This is frequently the single most overlooked factor in claiming decisions, and it's a major reason this book devotes entire chapters to spousal and survivor benefits rather than treating the claiming-age decision purely as an individual math problem.

The Emotional Side of This Decision

It's worth naming something that spreadsheets don't capture well: for many people, claiming Social Security carries an emotional and psychological dimension that goes beyond the numbers. Some people feel they've "earned" their benefit through decades of payroll taxes and want to start receiving it as soon as they're eligible, regardless of the math — and that is a legitimate value to weigh, not something to be talked out of. Others feel a strong pull toward maximizing lifetime value and find real peace of mind in a larger guaranteed check later in life. Neither instinct is wrong. The goal of understanding the mechanics in this book is to make sure that whichever instinct you lean toward, you're making that choice with clear eyes about what you're trading, rather than by accident or under time pressure.

A Practical Middle Ground

Not every household needs to choose between the extremes of 62 and 70. Claiming at your FRA is itself a reasonable middle path — full benefit, no reduction, no need to wait further, and no earnings test to navigate. For households that want simplicity and don't have a strong reason to lean toward either the earliest or latest end of the range, FRA claiming remains a perfectly sound default. There is no rule that says you must optimize to the exact month — a decision that feels comfortable and sustainable for your household is a legitimate goal in itself.

The "Bridge" Strategy: Using Savings to Fund a Delay

For households that want the larger, delayed benefit but don't have ongoing income to comfortably cover the gap years, one commonly discussed approach is a "bridge" strategy: using savings or investment withdrawals to cover living expenses during the years between leaving the workforce and claiming Social Security, essentially treating those withdrawals as a stand-in for the Social Security income that will begin later, at a higher monthly amount.

The logic behind this approach is that the withdrawals during the bridge years are, in effect, "buying" a larger, permanently guaranteed, inflation-adjusted income stream for the remainder of retirement — money spent down earlier in exchange for a stronger income floor later. This can make particular sense for a household with a substantial portfolio and genuine concern about outliving their savings, since it directly converts a portion of market-exposed savings into guaranteed lifetime income.

Whether a bridge strategy makes sense for a given household depends heavily on portfolio size, other income sources, risk tolerance, and the specific claiming ages under consideration — this is a strategy that benefits significantly from being modeled out with an advisor who can look at your actual account balances and expected expenses, rather than adopted based on the general concept alone.

Sequence-of-Returns Risk and Why Guaranteed Income Matters More Early in Retirement

One of the more technical but genuinely important concepts connected to the claiming-age decision is something financial planners call sequence-of-returns risk. In simple terms: if you're drawing down an investment portfolio for income and the market performs poorly in the early years of that drawdown, the combination of withdrawals and losses can permanently damage the portfolio's ability to recover, even if the market later rebounds strongly — because you're withdrawing from a smaller base during the recovery. The same average return, experienced in a different order, can produce a very different outcome depending on when the poor years happen to fall relative to when you started withdrawing.

A larger guaranteed Social Security benefit, obtained through delayed claiming, reduces the portion of your annual expenses that need to come from portfolio withdrawals, which in turn reduces your exposure to sequence-of-returns risk specifically in the vulnerable early years of retirement. This is a more technical version of the "insurance" framing introduced earlier in this chapter, and it's a concept worth raising directly with a financial advisor if you have a meaningful portion of your retirement income planned to come from investment withdrawals.

What Happens If You Do Nothing

It's worth being explicit about a detail that trips some people up: Social Security retirement benefits are not paid automatically simply because you've become eligible. Unlike the automatic Medicare enrollment described in Chapter Eight for people already receiving Social Security, you generally need to actively file an application for retirement benefits, whichever age you choose. Reaching 62, or your FRA, or 70 does not itself trigger payments — you (or in some cases, a representative acting on your behalf) need to submit a claim, typically through your online "my Social Security" account, by phone, or in person at a local field office.

This matters because "doing nothing" doesn't default you into any particular claiming age — it simply means benefits don't start. If your intention is to delay claiming for the reasons discussed throughout this chapter, that's a deliberate, informed form of "doing nothing" for now. But if you're unsure or haven't thought it through, make sure you understand that reaching a milestone age doesn't start your benefit automatically — you'll need to take an active step when you're ready.

A Second Illustration: A Single Retiree Without a Spouse to Coordinate With

Much of the household-level discussion in this book focuses on married or formerly married readers, since spousal dynamics add real complexity. But it's worth pausing to consider a single retiree, since the calculation is, in some ways, more straightforward without a second person's claiming age and survivor implications to weigh.

Consider a hypothetical single retiree, Beatrice, who never married and has no spousal or survivor benefit considerations at all. For Beatrice, the claiming decision comes down more purely to the factors discussed in this chapter: her own health and family longevity, her other income and savings, her tax situation, and her personal comfort with the trade-off between a smaller benefit sooner and a larger one later. Without a household perspective to weigh, Beatrice's decision is, in one sense, simpler — but it still benefits from the same careful thinking about longevity insurance and portfolio sequencing described above, since those factors apply just as much to an individual as to a couple. The absence of a spouse doesn't remove the value of thinking the decision through carefully; it just removes one layer of the analysis.

Longevity Statistics, Used Sensibly

It's worth touching briefly on how to think about population-level longevity statistics without either dismissing them entirely or over-relying on them for an individual decision. Life expectancy figures published by government agencies and actuarial organizations describe averages and probabilities across large populations — they are genuinely useful for understanding broad trends (life expectancy at 65 is generally meaningfully longer than life expectancy at birth, for instance, since it already accounts for having survived past the years with higher earlier-life mortality risk), but they say very little with certainty about any one individual's actual remaining years.

A more useful way to use these statistics is probabilistic rather than predictive: rather than asking "how long will I live," which nobody can answer with confidence, it can help to ask "what's a reasonable range of outcomes I should plan around, and how well does my strategy hold up across that range?" A claiming strategy that works out reasonably well whether you live to 78 or to 95 is generally more robust than one that only works out well under a narrow, specific lifespan assumption. This kind of range-based thinking, rather than a single-point guess, tends to lead to steadier, more resilient decisions.

Annuities as a Complementary Tool, Not a Competing One

Because delayed Social Security functions, as described earlier in this chapter, like a form of longevity insurance, it's worth briefly noting how it relates to a similar tool some retirees consider: private annuities, which are insurance products that convert a lump sum into guaranteed periodic income, often for life. Delayed Social Security and a private annuity share the same basic insurance logic — trading a lump sum or reduced near-term income for guaranteed income later — but Social Security's delayed credits are widely regarded by many financial planners as an unusually favorable version of this trade, in part because of the built-in inflation protection through COLA (described in Chapter One) and the absence of the fees, commissions, or insurer credit risk that can accompany some private annuity products.

This isn't a suggestion to avoid annuities altogether — they can play a legitimate role in some retirement plans, particularly for covering essential expenses beyond what Social Security and other guaranteed income sources provide. It's simply worth understanding that maximizing your delayed Social Security credits, where feasible for your household, is often one of the most efficient ways to build guaranteed lifetime income before considering supplemental annuity products for any remaining income gap — a sequencing point worth discussing with a financial advisor if annuities are part of your broader retirement income conversation.

Revisiting the Decision if the Rules Themselves Change

Because this chapter has emphasized that the claiming-age trade-off is built around actuarial assumptions and formulas set by current law, it's worth acknowledging directly that those formulas are not guaranteed to remain exactly as described forever. Social Security's long-term financing has been the subject of ongoing public discussion for decades, and it's reasonable to expect that Congress may, at some point, adjust aspects of the program — as it has periodically throughout the program's history, including as recently as the Social Security Fairness Act covered in Chapter Ten. This isn't a reason for alarm, and nothing in this book suggests dramatic changes are imminent or should drive a rushed decision. It's simply a reason to treat your claiming strategy as something to periodically revisit against current law, rather than a calculation you perform once, based on today's rules, and then assume will remain perfectly accurate regardless of how the underlying law might evolve over the years between now and when you actually claim.

Bringing Chapter Two and Chapter Three Together

Chapters Two and Three, taken together, are meant to give you both the mechanical facts (how much your benefit changes at each age, covered in Chapter Two) and the conceptual framework for weighing those facts against your own circumstances (the insurance framing, longevity considerations, and household dimension covered in this chapter). Neither chapter alone is sufficient for a good decision — the mechanics without the framework can lead to a narrow, spreadsheet-only view that misses important personal factors, while the framework without the mechanics leaves you reasoning about a decision without a clear sense of the actual numbers involved. Chapter Eleven will bring both of these together into a concrete, step-by-step process once the remaining chapters have added the spousal, survivor, tax, and Medicare dimensions this decision also depends on.

A Note on Inflation and Why "Today's Dollars" Framing Helps

Throughout this chapter and the last, comparisons between claiming ages have deliberately avoided specific dollar figures, in part because of the inflation caveat raised throughout this book, but it's worth explaining briefly why thinking in "today's dollars" is a useful mental habit even when you do eventually run your own numbers. Because Social Security benefits are adjusted for inflation through COLA once you're receiving them, and because the delayed-credit and early-reduction percentages are applied to your own Primary Insurance Amount rather than to a fixed historical dollar figure, comparing claiming ages in terms of today's purchasing power (rather than trying to project future nominal dollar amounts decades out, which involves guessing at future inflation) tends to produce a clearer, more stable picture. When you pull your own estimates from ssa.gov, you'll typically see them presented in today's dollars for exactly this reason — it's a more meaningful comparison than trying to estimate what a dollar will be worth in twenty years.

A Final Distinction: Risk Tolerance Versus Risk Capacity

Financial planners often distinguish between risk tolerance (how comfortable you feel, emotionally, with uncertainty) and risk capacity (how much financial uncertainty your actual resources can absorb without jeopardizing your basic needs). This distinction applies directly to the claiming-age decision: someone might feel emotionally comfortable delaying claiming and living off savings for several years (high risk tolerance), but if their savings are genuinely insufficient to support that gap safely (low risk capacity), that comfort level doesn't change the practical constraint. Conversely, someone might feel anxious about delaying even though their financial resources could easily support it (low risk tolerance despite high risk capacity). Being honest with yourself about which of these is actually driving your inclination — genuine financial constraint, or simply discomfort with delayed gratification — is a useful exercise before finalizing a claiming-age decision, since the two call for different responses: a real capacity constraint may mean claiming earlier is the right practical choice, while a tolerance issue might be better addressed by working through the insurance framing in this chapter more fully, rather than by claiming earlier than your actual resources would require.

A Summary Comparison to Carry Forward

To close this chapter, it may help to hold the two claiming philosophies side by side one final time. Claiming earlier trades a smaller monthly amount for more total years of payments, provides income sooner when it may be needed, and reduces exposure to the risk of never living long enough to benefit from delaying — but it also means a permanently smaller income floor, less protection against outliving other resources, and a smaller base for any eventual survivor benefit if you're the higher earner in a couple. Delaying trades near-term income for a larger, permanently higher monthly amount, functions as insurance against a long lifespan, and (for the higher earner in a couple) builds a larger survivor benefit floor — but it requires bridging the gap years through other resources and carries the risk of receiving less total value if life is shorter than average. Neither list is longer or more important than the other in the abstract; the right choice depends entirely on which set of trade-offs fits your own circumstances, which is exactly what the rest of this book is designed to help you evaluate.

Key Takeaways

Claiming early versus delaying is best understood as a trade-off between income shape and risk protection, not simply as "losing" or "gaining" money — total lifetime benefits can be similar for someone who lives an average lifespan.

Delaying functions like longevity insurance: it protects against the risk of living a long time and running short of other resources, at the cost of smaller or no payments in the earlier years.

For married couples, the claiming decision of the higher earner often shapes the eventual survivor benefit for the surviving spouse, adding a household dimension that pure individual break-even math misses.

There is no universally correct claiming age. FRA claiming remains a reasonable, simple middle path for households without a strong reason to lean toward either extreme.

Chapter Four: How Spousal Benefits Really Work

If you are married, Social Security offers something beyond your own individual retirement benefit: the possibility of a spousal benefit, based on your spouse's earnings record rather than your own. This chapter explains how spousal benefits are calculated, who qualifies, and the common misunderstandings that trip people up.

The Basic Structure

A spousal benefit allows one spouse to receive a benefit based on the other spouse's work record — up to 50% of that spouse's Primary Insurance Amount, if the spousal benefit claimant waits until their own FRA to claim it. This exists to protect spouses who earned less over their working lives, or who did not work in paid employment covered by Social Security at all, such as a spouse who spent years as a homemaker or primary caregiver.

Importantly, spousal benefits are not "extra" on top of your own retirement benefit if you also worked and qualify for a benefit on your own record. Instead, Social Security compares the two, and you effectively receive whichever is higher — your own benefit, or the spousal benefit calculated from your spouse's record. If your own benefit is already higher than 50% of your spouse's PIA, the spousal benefit provision doesn't add anything for you; if your own benefit is lower, you receive a combination that brings your total up to the spousal benefit amount.

Who Qualifies

To claim a spousal benefit, you generally need to be married to someone who is themselves entitled to retirement or disability benefits, and you generally need to be at least 62 years old (there are exceptions if you are caring for a qualifying child). The marriage generally needs to have lasted at least one year at the time of application, with some exceptions.

One detail that surprises people: your spouse does not necessarily need to have already claimed their own benefit in every circumstance, but historically, under current rules, your spouse generally does need to have filed for their own retirement benefit before you can claim a spousal benefit based on their record (this differs from divorced-spouse rules, covered in the next chapter, which can be more flexible). Because these filing-sequence rules are exactly the kind of detail that can change or that varies by specific circumstance, this is a case where confirming the current rule directly with the SSA before you apply is especially worthwhile.

The FRA Reduction Applies Here Too

Just as with your own retirement benefit, claiming a spousal benefit before your own FRA results in a permanent reduction — though the reduction schedule for spousal benefits is calculated somewhat differently from the schedule for your own retirement benefit, generally resulting in a maximum spousal benefit of 50% of the other spouse's PIA if you claim at your own FRA, and a lower percentage if you claim earlier than that.

One important and frequently misunderstood point: delayed retirement credits do not apply to spousal benefits. Waiting past your own FRA does not increase your spousal benefit percentage beyond that FRA-level maximum of 50%. This is a meaningful difference from your own retirement benefit, where waiting past FRA continues to increase your amount up to age 70. If you are planning to rely primarily on a spousal benefit, there is generally no additional financial benefit to delaying your claim past your own FRA — though your spouse's own decision about when to claim their retirement benefit still matters, since your spousal benefit is a percentage of their PIA regardless of when you personally claim it.

The Deemed Filing Rule

In the past, some people used a strategy of claiming only a spousal benefit while letting their own retirement benefit continue growing with delayed credits, then switching to their own larger benefit later. For most people born after January 1, 1954, this strategy is no longer available: under what's called "deemed filing," when you apply for either your own retirement benefit or a spousal benefit, you are generally deemed to be applying for both, and you receive whichever is higher — you can't selectively claim just one while letting the other grow. A narrow exception may still apply to people born before that date, but this affects a shrinking share of new claimants each year, and again is worth confirming with the SSA for your specific birth year.

An Illustration

Consider a hypothetical couple: Harold and Ines. Harold worked steadily throughout his career and has a healthy earnings record. Ines worked part-time for many years while raising their children and later returned to full-time work but for a shorter overall span, resulting in a modest benefit on her own record — meaningfully lower than 50% of Harold's PIA.

When Ines reaches her own FRA, she is eligible to receive the higher of her own benefit or a spousal benefit worth up to 50% of Harold's PIA (assuming Harold has already filed for his own benefit). Because her own record produces a lower number, she effectively receives a combination that brings her total up to that spousal amount. She does not receive her own benefit plus the spousal benefit stacked on top — she receives the larger of the two figures, blended through the calculation SSA performs automatically.

This is one of the most common points of confusion for people learning about spousal benefits for the first time: it is not additive. It is a "floor" that brings a lower-earning spouse's benefit up to a share of the higher earner's benefit, not a bonus paid on top of an otherwise complete benefit.

Why the Higher Earner's Claiming Age Still Matters

Even though delaying past your own FRA doesn't increase your spousal benefit percentage, the higher earner's claiming decision still indirectly matters to the household, for two reasons. First, the spousal benefit is calculated as a percentage of the higher earner's PIA — the number calculated at their own FRA — regardless of when the higher earner actually claims. Second, and more significantly, the higher earner's claiming age has a major effect on the eventual survivor benefit, which we cover in the next chapter. A couple thinking through their combined strategy should generally weigh the higher earner's claiming decision with the survivor benefit implications in mind, not just the spousal benefit implications, since the survivor benefit is often the larger and more consequential number over the long run.

A Note on Same-Sex Marriages

Following the Supreme Court's 2015 recognition of same-sex marriage nationwide, spousal and survivor benefits generally apply equally regardless of the sex of the spouses, following the same rules described throughout this book. If you have questions about how your specific marriage history interacts with these rules — including marriages that occurred before certain legal recognitions were in place in particular states — the SSA can review your specific circumstances directly.

When Both Spouses Have Substantial Earnings Records

The examples used so far in this chapter mostly describe a couple with a clear higher earner and a clear lower earner. But an increasing share of couples reach retirement with two substantial, relatively similar earnings records, having both worked full careers. It's worth being clear about how spousal benefits function in that situation: if your own retirement benefit, based on your own record, is already higher than 50% of your spouse's PIA, the spousal benefit provision simply doesn't add anything for you — you receive your own benefit, full stop, with no spousal top-up involved.

This is worth stating plainly because some people assume that being married automatically entitles them to some kind of spousal boost regardless of their own earnings record, which isn't accurate. Spousal benefits exist specifically to bring a lower-earning spouse's benefit up toward a share of the higher earner's amount — for two spouses with comparably strong records, the spousal provision typically has little or no practical effect, and each spouse's own claiming-age decision, following the logic of Chapters Two and Three, becomes the primary driver of their own benefit.

What to Expect When You Apply for a Spousal Benefit

The practical process of applying for a spousal benefit involves confirming your marriage (generally through a marriage certificate or similar documentation), confirming your own identity and work history, and confirming your spouse's entitlement to their own benefit. If you're applying online or by phone, the SSA will generally walk you through what documentation is needed based on your specific circumstances — it's rarely a fully self-service process for spousal claims the way a straightforward individual retirement claim can sometimes be, simply because there are more moving pieces to verify.

Because spousal benefit amounts depend directly on your spouse's PIA, it's worth having a general sense of your spouse's own claiming situation and estimated benefit before you apply, so the numbers you're told make sense in context. If your spouse hasn't yet filed for their own benefit, remember from earlier in this chapter that, for most married couples under current rules, that generally needs to happen before your spousal benefit based on their record can begin.

How Non-Covered Government Work Complicates Spousal Benefits

If your spouse spent part of their career in a job that didn't pay into Social Security — a topic covered in much greater depth in Chapter Ten — this historically could reduce or eliminate spousal benefits available to the other spouse under a provision called the Government Pension Offset (GPO). As discussed in Chapter Ten, GPO was repealed by the Social Security Fairness Act in January 2025, which changed this significantly for many affected couples going forward. If you or your spouse have any history of non-covered government work, it's worth reading Chapter Ten closely and following up directly with the SSA, since this can meaningfully change what you're entitled to compared to what you may have been told in the past.

Common Spousal Benefit Mistakes

A frequent point of confusion is assuming spousal benefits stack on top of your own retirement benefit rather than functioning as a "floor" that brings your total up to the higher of the two amounts, as explained earlier in this chapter — this is worth re-reading if it didn't fully click the first time, since it changes the entire way you should think about the value of a spousal claim.

Another common mistake is assuming that delaying your own claim past your own FRA will increase your spousal benefit the way it increases a retirement benefit. As covered above, it does not — delayed retirement credits don't apply to spousal benefits, so there's generally no reason, from a spousal-benefit-maximizing perspective alone, to delay your own claim past your own FRA if you expect to end up relying primarily on the spousal benefit.

A third mistake is not considering the survivor benefit implications, covered in the next chapter, when thinking through the higher earner's claiming strategy. Because the spousal benefit is capped at 50% of the higher earner's PIA regardless of when the higher earner claims, but the eventual survivor benefit is directly shaped by the higher earner's claiming age, the two benefits pull in somewhat different directions when it comes to optimizing the higher earner's decision — a tension worth understanding fully before finalizing a household strategy, which Chapter Eleven will help you work through systematically.

Walking Through the Percentages Without Specific Dollar Figures

Because percentages can still be a bit abstract without a concrete walk-through, consider the following purely illustrative pattern, using placeholder relative values rather than real dollar figures, to make the mechanics clearer.

Suppose one spouse's own retirement benefit at their FRA would replace a certain share of their pre-retirement income, and the other spouse — who earned significantly less over their career — has an own-record benefit that comes to well under half of the higher earner's FRA benefit. In that case, the lower-earning spouse's spousal benefit, calculated as up to 50% of the higher earner's PIA, would exceed their own individual benefit, meaning they'd receive the spousal-based amount rather than their own smaller benefit, following the "higher of the two" rule explained earlier in this chapter.

Now suppose instead that the lower-earning spouse's own benefit already comes to, say, 60% of the higher earner's PIA — comfortably above the 50% spousal ceiling. In that case, their own benefit already exceeds what the spousal provision could offer them, and the spousal benefit provision effectively provides no additional value, since SSA pays whichever amount is higher, and their own record already wins that comparison. The exact crossover point — where a spouse's own benefit stops being lower than the spousal amount and starts being higher — is always the same 50%-of-the-higher-earner's-PIA threshold, regardless of the actual dollar figures involved, which is why understanding the percentage relationship matters more than trying to memorize specific dollar examples that will change over time anyway.

How the Application Process Works in Practice

When you apply for retirement benefits and you're married, the SSA's application process generally evaluates both your own-record benefit and any spousal benefit you might be eligible for as part of the same overall process, rather than requiring two entirely separate applications in most cases — though the specific paperwork can vary depending on your circumstances, particularly if your spouse hasn't yet filed for their own benefit, since as covered earlier in this chapter, their filing status generally affects your spousal eligibility. It's generally efficient to apply for both your own retirement benefit and any potential spousal benefit at the same time, disclosing your marital status and spouse's information during the application, so the SSA can determine and pay you the higher of the two amounts without requiring a separate follow-up application later. If your circumstances change after you've filed — for instance, if your spouse claims their own benefit for the first time after you've already claimed yours — it's worth proactively checking with the SSA about whether that changes your own spousal eligibility, rather than assuming the system will automatically flag it for you.

Spousal Benefits When One Spouse Has a Non-Covered Pension

As briefly noted earlier in this chapter, and as covered in much greater depth in Chapter Ten, if the spouse whose record you'd be claiming against has a pension from work that didn't pay into Social Security, historically the Government Pension Offset provision reduced or eliminated spousal benefits available to the other spouse — not because of anything about the claiming spouse's own record, but because of the record-holder's non-covered pension in certain configurations of this rule. Following the Social Security Fairness Act's repeal of GPO in January 2025, this offset generally no longer applies going forward. If either you or your spouse has any history of non-covered government work, this is directly relevant to your spousal benefit planning, and it's worth reading Chapter Ten in full before finalizing your household's strategy, since the financial difference between the pre-repeal and post-repeal treatment can be substantial.

What Happens to Spousal Benefits If the Marriage Ends After You've Already Claimed

If you're already receiving a spousal benefit and your marriage later ends in divorce, your ongoing eligibility generally shifts from the current-spouse spousal benefit rules described throughout this chapter to the divorced-spouse rules described in Chapter Six, which, as that chapter explains, actually offer somewhat more flexibility in some respects (such as not depending on your ex-spouse's filing status, once you've been divorced at least two years). If this situation applies to you, it's worth proactively contacting the SSA to understand how your specific benefit transitions, rather than assuming your existing spousal benefit simply continues unchanged or is automatically lost — in most cases where the marriage lasted the requisite 10 years, your eligibility continues in a modified form under the divorced-spouse provisions rather than ending outright.

Tying Spousal Benefits Back to the Household Perspective

This chapter has focused on the mechanics of spousal benefits in isolation, but it's worth restating the broader point this book returns to repeatedly: a spousal benefit is rarely the whole story for a married couple. The higher earner's own claiming decision, covered in Chapters Two and Three, the eventual survivor benefit that decision shapes, covered in Chapter Five, and the spousal benefit covered in this chapter are three interlocking pieces of the same household strategy, not three separate, independent decisions. A couple that optimizes each piece in isolation — the higher earner claiming purely for their own break-even age, the lower earner claiming a spousal benefit purely for their own convenience, without looking at how the pieces fit together — often leaves value on the table compared to a couple that works through all three chapters together and makes a coordinated household decision. Chapter Eleven will give you a structured way to do exactly that.

A Note on Discussing This With Your Spouse

Because spousal benefits, by definition, involve two people's financial futures, it's worth saying something directly about the conversation itself, not just the mechanics. Some couples find claiming-age discussions straightforward; others find that differing risk tolerances, differing assumptions about health and longevity, or simply differing comfort levels with financial planning in general can make this a harder conversation than the math alone would suggest. If that's true in your household, it may help to separate the conversation into two distinct steps: first, making sure you both understand the mechanics covered in this book (perhaps by reading the same chapters and discussing them section by section, rather than one spouse researching alone and summarizing conclusions to the other), and second, actually weighing the trade-offs together once you're both working from the same factual foundation. Couples who reach a joint claiming strategy through this kind of shared understanding, rather than one spouse simply deferring to the other's conclusion, tend to report more confidence in the decision after it's made.

A Quick Reference for This Chapter's Key Numbers

To close this chapter, it may help to have its central percentages summarized together. A spousal benefit can reach up to 50% of the higher earner's PIA, but only if claimed at the lower earner's own FRA — claiming earlier reduces that percentage, and delaying past FRA does not increase it, since delayed retirement credits don't apply to spousal benefits. You always receive the higher of your own benefit or the spousal amount, never both added together. And under deemed filing rules that apply to most current claimants, applying for one type of benefit generally applies you for both simultaneously, with SSA automatically paying whichever is higher. Holding these four points together gives you the essential mental model for spousal benefits, even before you have your own or your spouse's specific dollar figures in hand.

Key Takeaways

A spousal benefit can provide up to 50% of your spouse's Primary Insurance Amount if you claim it at your own FRA, but you receive the higher of your own benefit or the spousal benefit — not both added together.

Claiming a spousal benefit before your own FRA permanently reduces it, but delaying past your own FRA does not increase it — delayed retirement credits do not apply to spousal benefits.

Under deemed filing rules that apply to most current claimants, applying for one benefit type (your own or spousal) generally applies you for both, with SSA paying the higher amount — the "claim spousal, delay your own" strategy is largely unavailable to people born in 1954 or later.

The higher earner's own claiming age still matters to the household overall, primarily because of its large effect on the eventual survivor benefit, covered in the next chapter.

Chapter Five: Survivor Benefits: What Widows and Widowers Need to Know

Of all the benefit categories covered in this book, survivor benefits are arguably the most consequential and the most under-discussed. They determine what happens to a surviving spouse's income after the death of a husband or wife, and the decisions made years earlier — by both spouses, about their own claiming ages — directly shape what that survivor benefit will be. This chapter explains the mechanics clearly, because the stakes here are high and the rules are genuinely different from spousal benefits, not just a variation on them.

The Core Concept

When a person who was entitled to Social Security benefits dies, their surviving spouse may become eligible for a survivor benefit based on the deceased spouse's record. Unlike a spousal benefit — which tops out at 50% of the other spouse's PIA — a survivor benefit can be worth up to 100% of what the deceased spouse was receiving (or was entitled to receive) at the time of death, if the survivor claims it at their own FRA.

This distinction matters enormously. It means the claiming decision the higher-earning spouse makes during their own lifetime doesn't just affect their own monthly check — it effectively sets the ceiling for what their surviving spouse can eventually receive as a survivor benefit.

How the Deceased Spouse's Claiming Age Echoes Forward

If the higher-earning spouse claimed their own retirement benefit early, before their FRA, their monthly benefit was permanently reduced — and that reduced amount (not their full PIA) generally becomes the base amount available to the survivor, subject to survivor-specific rules. If the higher-earning spouse instead delayed claiming past their own FRA and earned delayed retirement credits, that larger amount generally becomes the base the survivor can eventually receive.

This is the mechanism referenced in earlier chapters: when a higher-earning spouse in a couple delays their own claim, they are not only building a larger benefit for themselves — they are also, in effect, building a larger financial floor for their spouse in the event that they pass away first. For couples where one spouse significantly out-earned the other over their careers, this single fact often carries more financial weight than almost any other claiming consideration in this book, because a surviving spouse — often a woman, statistically, given typical life expectancy gaps — may live for many years, sometimes decades, relying substantially on that survivor benefit as a primary income source.

When Survivor Benefits Can Begin

Survivor benefits can generally begin as early as age 60 (age 50 if the surviving spouse is disabled), which is notably earlier than the earliest age for retirement or spousal benefits.

As with other benefit types, claiming a survivor benefit before the survivor's own FRA results in a reduction, and claiming at the survivor's FRA provides the full amount available (up to 100% of the deceased spouse's benefit). Unlike retirement benefits, there are no delayed credits for waiting past FRA to claim a survivor benefit specifically — the maximum is reached at the survivor's own FRA.

A Valuable and Often-Missed Flexibility: Claiming Sequence

One of the more useful, lesser-known features of the system is that a surviving spouse who is eligible for both a survivor benefit and their own retirement benefit does not have to claim both at the same time or in the same way. In many cases, a surviving spouse can strategically claim one type of benefit first — for example, their own reduced retirement benefit at a younger age, while allowing the survivor benefit to grow toward its maximum at their own FRA (or vice versa, depending on which benefit is larger and how each grows) — and then switch to the other benefit later. Unlike the "deemed filing" restriction on spousal benefits described in the previous chapter, survivor benefits generally are not subject to the same deemed-filing rule, which preserves more flexibility for widows and widowers to sequence their claims strategically.

Because the specific rules around this sequencing depend on your exact circumstances, and can be genuinely intricate, this is one of the areas of Social Security planning where speaking directly with the SSA or a financial advisor experienced in survivor benefits is particularly worthwhile — the difference in lifetime income between an optimal and a suboptimal sequencing decision can be substantial.

An Illustration

Consider a hypothetical widow, Patricia, age 61, whose husband recently passed away. Patricia has her own modest retirement benefit available starting at 62, and she is also eligible for a survivor benefit based on her late husband's record, which would be larger if she waits until her own FRA to claim it.

One path available to Patricia: claim her own smaller retirement benefit early (accepting the permanent reduction on that smaller benefit specifically), while allowing her survivor benefit to continue growing toward its maximum, then switch to the larger survivor benefit once she reaches her own FRA. Because her own retirement benefit and her survivor benefit are calculated somewhat independently in terms of timing, this sequencing can allow her to receive some income sooner while still eventually accessing the larger survivor amount at full value.

Whether this sequencing makes sense for any individual depends on the specific numbers involved — the size of the personal benefit versus the survivor benefit, the household's need for immediate income, health considerations, and other resources available. This is exactly the kind of situation where running the numbers with an SSA representative or financial advisor, rather than guessing, pays off.

Remarriage and Survivor Benefits

Remarriage can affect eligibility for survivor benefits, but the rules are more forgiving than many people assume. Generally, if you remarry before age 60 (or before 50 if disabled), you may not be able to collect survivor benefits on your former spouse's record while that later marriage continues. However, if you remarry at age 60 or later, that remarriage generally does not prevent you from receiving survivor benefits based on your earlier, deceased spouse's record. This distinction — the age-60 threshold — surprises many people who assume any remarriage cancels survivor eligibility outright. It doesn't, as long as the remarriage happens at or after that age.

Survivor Benefits for Children

While the primary focus of this book is retirement-age claiming, it's worth noting briefly that survivor benefits can also be available to dependent children of a deceased worker, generally until age 18 (or longer if the child remains a full-time student in secondary school up to a certain age, or indefinitely if the child has a qualifying disability that began before adulthood). Families navigating the loss of a working parent with dependent children should raise this directly with the SSA, since eligibility and amounts depend on specific family circumstances beyond the scope of this general guide.

The Survivor Benefit Reduction Schedule in More Detail

Just as with retirement and spousal benefits, claiming a survivor benefit before your own FRA results in a reduction, but the survivor reduction schedule is calculated somewhat differently from the retirement-benefit reduction schedule described in Chapter Two. Broadly speaking, claiming a survivor benefit at the earliest available age (60, or 50 if disabled) results in a survivor benefit meaningfully below the full amount, with the reduction gradually shrinking as you approach your own FRA, at which point you receive the full survivor amount (up to 100% of what the deceased spouse was entitled to). Because the exact percentage reduction at each age depends on your own FRA and the current formula, this is an area where an SSA representative can give you a precise, personalized figure far more reliably than any general description.

Practical Steps for Applying for Survivor Benefits

Applying for survivor benefits generally requires documentation of the death (typically a death certificate, though the SSA is often notified directly by a funeral home in many cases, which can simplify this step), documentation of your marriage, and your own identifying information. It's generally advisable to contact the SSA relatively soon after a spouse's death, both because certain benefits (including a modest one-time death payment available to some survivors) may have specific application windows, and because ongoing monthly survivor benefits generally are not paid retroactively for periods before you apply, beyond certain limited retroactive windows — meaning that delaying your application unnecessarily can mean permanently missing out on payments for the delayed months, separate from the claiming-age reduction discussed above.

That said, this doesn't mean you need to rush a decision about which benefit to claim first (your own retirement benefit or your survivor benefit, per the sequencing discussion above) in the immediate aftermath of a loss — it means initiating contact with the SSA promptly is worthwhile, even if you take additional time to decide on the specific claiming strategy once you understand your options.

Survivor Benefits and the Timing of a Later Remarriage

Because remarriage before age 60 generally ends eligibility for survivor benefits based on a deceased spouse's record (while that later marriage continues), and remarriage at 60 or later generally does not, this age threshold occasionally becomes a genuine, practical consideration for a widow or widower who is contemplating remarriage and is aware of a meaningful survivor benefit available to them. This is obviously a deeply personal decision that goes well beyond financial considerations, and nothing in this book is meant to suggest that financial factors should outweigh personal ones. It is simply worth knowing that this threshold exists, so that if remarriage timing is already a topic under discussion for other reasons, the financial dimension can be factored in with accurate information rather than a vague sense that "remarrying will cost me my benefits," which, as described above, is not automatically true if the remarriage happens at 60 or later.

A Second Illustration: A Widower Considering His Options

Consider a hypothetical widower, Desmond, age 63, whose wife passed away recently after a long career with a significantly higher earnings record than his own. Desmond is eligible for his own modest retirement benefit now, and would be eligible for a substantially larger survivor benefit based on his late wife's record — a benefit that would reach its maximum value at his own FRA of 66 and a few months.

Desmond has a choice similar to the one described earlier for Patricia: he could claim his own smaller retirement benefit now, accepting its permanent reduction for claiming a few years before his own FRA, while allowing his survivor benefit to continue toward its larger, unreduced value at his FRA — then switch to the survivor benefit once he reaches that age. Alternatively, depending on his specific numbers and income needs, a different sequence might make more sense. Because his late wife's benefit was significantly higher than his own, and because the survivor benefit calculation in his case is likely to represent the larger share of his future household income, this is exactly the kind of situation where a detailed conversation with the SSA — bringing both benefit estimates to the table — is worth the time it takes, given how much is at stake in getting the sequencing right.

The Lump-Sum Death Benefit

Separate from ongoing monthly survivor benefits, a modest one-time lump-sum death payment may be available to an eligible surviving spouse (or, in some circumstances, an eligible surviving child) upon the death of a worker who had accumulated sufficient work credits. This payment is generally quite small relative to ongoing monthly benefits and is not intended to function as life insurance or meaningful financial support on its own — it's a narrow, specific benefit worth being aware of primarily so you know to ask about it when contacting the SSA after a spouse's death, rather than a payment substantial enough to factor significantly into broader financial planning.

Survivor Benefits for a Disabled Widow or Widower

If a surviving spouse is disabled, survivor benefits may be available starting earlier than the standard age-60 threshold described earlier in this chapter — generally as early as age 50, provided the disability began within a certain period relative to the worker's death and meets Social Security's disability criteria, which are evaluated separately from the survivor benefit eligibility itself. Because disability determinations involve their own detailed medical and vocational evaluation process, a surviving spouse who believes they may qualify under this provision should contact the SSA directly to begin that evaluation, rather than assuming eligibility either way based on general descriptions like this one.

How Survivor Benefits Interact With a Government Pension

Just as spousal benefits can be affected by a recipient's own non-covered government pension through the Government Pension Offset described in Chapter Ten, survivor benefits were historically subject to the same GPO provision. If you receive, or expect to receive, a pension from work that didn't pay into Social Security, and you're also eligible for a survivor benefit based on a spouse's or former spouse's Social Security record, this is directly relevant to you — and, as covered in Chapter Ten, the repeal of GPO through the Social Security Fairness Act in January 2025 changed this significantly for affected survivors going forward. If this describes your situation, reading Chapter Ten in full, and following up with the SSA about your specific case, is well worth the time, since the financial difference between the old and new treatment can be substantial for someone in this position.

Notifying the SSA and Coordinating With Other Benefits After a Death

Beyond the Social Security-specific steps described earlier in this chapter, the death of a spouse often triggers a cascade of administrative tasks — notifying pension administrators, life insurance companies, banks, and other institutions, in addition to the

SSA. It's worth understanding that Social Security survivor benefits are handled entirely separately from these other institutions; providing a death certificate to a pension administrator, for instance, does not automatically notify the SSA, and vice versa. Each institution generally needs to be contacted and provided documentation independently. Some funeral homes offer to report a death to the SSA as part of their services, which can be a helpful head start, but it's still worth confirming directly with the SSA that this notification was received and that your own survivor benefit application has been properly initiated, rather than assuming it happened automatically.

Coordinating Survivor Benefits With Life Insurance and Other Death Benefits

It's worth understanding that Social Security survivor benefits are calculated and paid independently of any life insurance proceeds, pension survivor benefits, or other death benefits a surviving spouse might receive — one does not reduce or offset the other in the way that, for instance, a spousal benefit and your own retirement benefit interact with each other, as described in Chapter Four. This is generally good news for a grieving family navigating a difficult time: the survivor benefit calculation described throughout this chapter operates on its own, based purely on the deceased spouse's Social Security record and the survivor's own age and claiming choices, without needing to account for what other death benefits may also be arriving from other sources.

Why This Chapter Deserves Careful Reading Even If Both Spouses Are Currently Healthy

It's natural to want to skip ahead past a chapter about widowhood when both spouses in a marriage are currently healthy and this topic feels distant. But the value of understanding survivor benefits in advance — rather than learning about them for the first time during a period of grief — is exactly why this chapter belongs earlier in your planning process, not later. The claiming-age decision covered in Chapters Two and Three directly shapes the survivor benefit described in this chapter, which means understanding this chapter's mechanics is genuinely relevant input into a decision you might make years or decades before either spouse's death actually occurs. Revisiting this chapter specifically when working through Chapter Eleven's household planning steps, even while both spouses are in good health, is one of the more valuable applications of the material in this entire book.

A Quick Reference for This Chapter's Key Numbers

Survivor benefits can reach up to 100% of the deceased spouse's benefit (compared to a maximum of 50% for spousal benefits covered in the previous chapter), if claimed at the survivor's own FRA. They can begin as early as age 60 (50 if disabled) — earlier than any other benefit category covered in this book — with a reduction for claiming before the survivor's own FRA. The deceased spouse's own claiming age during their lifetime directly shapes the base amount available to the survivor: a reduced benefit from early claiming generally produces a smaller survivor base, while delayed retirement credits from waiting generally produce a larger one. And remarriage at 60 or later generally does not end eligibility for survivor benefits from an earlier deceased spouse, even though remarriage before 60 generally does, while that later marriage continues. These four points are the essential mental model for survivor benefits to carry into your own household planning.

Why This Chapter Often Carries the Most Financial Weight in the Book

Of every topic covered across these eleven chapters, survivor benefits arguably deserve the most attention relative to how little they're typically discussed, because the dollar stakes involved are frequently the largest of any single decision in this book. A household where the higher earner delayed claiming to 70 versus claimed at 62 can see a surviving spouse's monthly income differ substantially for what may be decades of widowhood — often the single largest financial consequence of any claiming-age choice covered in this book, larger in total lifetime impact than the difference in the higher earner's own benefit alone. If you take one piece of cross-chapter advice from this book above all others, let it be this: when working through Chapters Two and Three's claiming-age decision as a married couple, weigh the survivor-benefit consequences described in this chapter as seriously as you weigh either spouse's own individual break-even math, because for many households, this is where the real financial weight of the decision actually lives.

Key Takeaways

Survivor benefits can be worth up to 100% of the deceased spouse's benefit (compared to 50% for spousal benefits), making the higher earner's own claiming-age decision during their lifetime a major factor in what their surviving spouse can eventually receive.

Survivor benefits can begin as early as age 60 (50 if disabled), earlier than retirement or spousal benefits, with reductions for claiming before the survivor's own FRA.

Widows and widowers often have valuable flexibility to sequence their own retirement benefit and their survivor benefit differently, claiming one earlier and switching to the other later — this is an area where personalized guidance is especially valuable.

Remarriage at age 60 or later generally does not prevent collecting survivor benefits from an earlier deceased spouse's record, though remarriage before 60 generally does, while that marriage continues.

Chapter Six: Divorced? What You May Still Be Entitled To

Divorce ends a marriage, but for Social Security purposes, it does not always end your connection to your former spouse's earnings record. Many divorced people are unaware that they may still qualify for benefits based on an ex-spouse's work history — benefits that, in some respects, are more flexible than the spousal benefits available to currently married couples. This chapter explains how divorced-spouse and divorced-survivor benefits work.

Basic Eligibility for Divorced-Spouse Benefits

To qualify for a benefit based on an ex-spouse's record, several conditions generally need to be met: the marriage must have lasted at least 10 years, you must currently be unmarried (remarriage generally ends eligibility for benefits on a former spouse's record, subject to some of the same age-60-plus survivor exceptions discussed for widows and widowers in the previous chapter, which can apply to divorced survivor benefits as well), you must be at least 62 years old, and the benefit you'd receive based on your own record must be smaller than the divorced-spouse benefit you'd receive based on your ex-spouse's record.

The 10-year marriage threshold is a hard line — a marriage that lasted nine years and eleven months does not qualify, while one that lasted ten years and one month does. If you are approaching this threshold and considering the timing of a divorce, this is worth being aware of, though obviously this is a deeply personal decision that goes well beyond financial planning.

A Key Advantage Over Current-Spouse Benefits

Here is where divorced-spouse benefits differ meaningfully, and favorably, from the spousal benefit rules covered in Chapter Four: if you have been divorced for at least two years, you can generally claim a divorced-spouse benefit even if your ex-spouse has not yet filed for their own retirement benefit — as long as your ex-spouse is at least 62 and eligible to file, even if they haven't. This removes the dependency on your ex-spouse's own filing decision that applies to current spouses, which can matter a great deal if your ex-spouse is, for whatever reason, delaying their own claim or if you simply have no ongoing contact with them to coordinate timing.

Claiming a Divorced-Spouse Benefit Does Not Affect Your Ex-Spouse

Another detail that surprises people, and sometimes causes needless anxiety: if you claim a divorced-spouse benefit based on your ex-spouse's earnings record, it does not reduce your ex-spouse's own benefit, and it does not affect benefits available to your ex-spouse's current spouse, if they have remarried. Social Security can pay divorced-spouse benefits to multiple former spouses simultaneously, all based on the same worker's record, without any of them affecting each other or the worker's own benefit. This is a genuinely separate calculation for each qualifying claim.

Divorced-Spouse Benefits Follow the Same Percentage Structure

The percentage math for a divorced-spouse benefit mirrors the current-spouse rules from Chapter Four: up to 50% of your ex-spouse's PIA if you claim at your own FRA, reduced if you claim earlier, with no increase available for delaying past your own FRA (delayed credits don't apply here either), and deemed filing rules generally applying in a similar way for people born in 1954 or later.

Divorced-Survivor Benefits

If your ex-spouse passes away, you may be eligible for a divorced-survivor benefit, generally following the same structural rules as the survivor benefits described in Chapter Five — potentially up to 100% of what your ex-spouse was entitled to, available as early as age 60 (50 if disabled), with the same remarriage-at-60-or-later exception applying. The same 10-year marriage-length requirement applies, and you generally need to remain unmarried (or have remarried at 60 or later) to qualify.

Notably, if you were married to your ex-spouse for 10 years or more and they later remarried before passing away, both you and their subsequent spouse (assuming that marriage also meets eligibility rules) may separately qualify for survivor benefits on their record, without either claim reducing the other. This is a structural feature of the program that often surprises people navigating a blended-family situation.

Multiple Marriages of 10+ Years

If you were married more than once, each for at least 10 years, and are otherwise eligible, you can generally choose to claim a divorced-spouse or divorced-survivor benefit based on whichever former spouse's record produces the higher benefit for you, following the same "higher of your own or the derived benefit" logic described in earlier chapters.

An Illustration

Consider a hypothetical retiree, Julissa, who was married to her first husband for 14 years before divorcing, and never remarried. Her own earnings record, from a career interrupted several times, produces a modest benefit. Because her marriage exceeded the 10-year threshold, she is eligible to claim a divorced-spouse benefit based on her ex-husband's record once she turns 62 and he is at least 62 himself — regardless of whether he has actually filed for his own benefit yet, since they have been divorced well over two years. If her ex-husband later passes away, she would similarly be eligible to apply for a divorced-survivor benefit, following the same rules that would apply to a widow who had remained married.

Why This Chapter Matters Even If You Think It Doesn't Apply to You

Divorced-spouse and divorced-survivor benefits are widely underclaimed, largely because people assume divorce severed their connection to a former spouse's Social Security record entirely. If you were married for 10 years or more at any point in your life and are not currently remarried (or remarried at 60 or later), it is worth checking your eligibility directly with the SSA — even if you haven't thought about your ex-spouse's earnings record in years. This is a case where a few minutes of checking can reveal a meaningfully larger benefit than you assumed you were entitled to.

Documentation You'll Likely Need

Because divorced-spouse and divorced-survivor claims require the SSA to verify a marriage that may have ended many years or even decades earlier, it's worth gathering relevant documentation before you apply, if you can. This generally includes your marriage certificate, your divorce decree (which typically documents the length of the marriage and the date it legally ended), and your ex-spouse's Social Security number if you have it, along with their name and approximate date of birth. If you don't have your ex-spouse's Social Security number, the SSA can often still locate their record using other identifying information, though having it on hand tends to simplify and speed up the process considerably.

If your divorce occurred a very long time ago and locating paperwork feels daunting, it's worth checking with your local county or state vital records office, which typically maintains copies of marriage and divorce records that can be requested even many years later.

What If You Don't Know Your Ex-Spouse's Current Whereabouts

A common concern people raise is not knowing where a former spouse currently lives, whether they're still alive, or details about their current earnings or benefit status. It's worth knowing that none of this is generally required for you to apply for a divorced-spouse or divorced-survivor benefit — the SSA can access the necessary information about your ex-spouse's record internally once you've provided your marriage documentation and identifying details, without you needing to track them down or coordinate with them directly. This is one of the more privacy-preserving aspects of the divorced-spouse benefit system: your ex-spouse is not notified that you've applied for a benefit based on their record, and as covered above, your claim doesn't reduce what they receive.

Multiple Marriages of Ten or More Years, in More Detail

For readers who have been married more than once, each time for ten years or longer, it's worth understanding how the SSA approaches the choice among former spouses. Generally, you are not required to guess which former spouse's record would produce a higher benefit for you — the SSA can help evaluate your options against each qualifying former spouse's record, and you can generally choose to claim against whichever produces the higher amount for you, following the standard "higher of your own or the derived benefit" logic described throughout this book. If your circumstances involve multiple qualifying former marriages, it's especially worth having a direct conversation with the SSA rather than trying to estimate this comparison on your own, since it depends on details (like each former spouse's specific earnings history) that aren't something you're likely to have precise visibility into from home.

Common Misconceptions About Divorced-Spouse Benefits

A frequent misconception is that claiming a divorced-spouse benefit somehow requires your ex-spouse's permission or cooperation. As described above, this generally is not the case — the benefit is calculated and paid based on SSA's own records, without requiring your ex-spouse's involvement or consent.

A second misconception is that divorced-spouse benefits are somehow a "lesser" or less legitimate category of benefit compared to current-spouse benefits. Structurally, they follow essentially the same percentage rules (up to 50% of the ex-spouse's PIA for a divorced-spousal benefit, up to 100% for a divorced-survivor benefit), simply extended to marriages that ended in divorce rather than continuing until death, as long as the ten-year threshold and other eligibility requirements described above are met.

A third misconception, understandable but incorrect, is assuming that because your own individual retirement benefit exists, you're not eligible to also check for a potentially larger divorced-spouse benefit. As covered throughout this book, SSA automatically pays you the higher of the two amounts you're eligible for — there's no reason not to check, and no downside to confirming your eligibility even if you assume your own benefit is likely to be larger.

Same-Sex Divorced Couples and Historical Marriage Recognition

For same-sex couples whose marriage occurred before nationwide recognition of same-sex marriage in 2015, but who were legally married in a state that recognized such marriages earlier, or whose relationship involved a long-term partnership that only later became a legally recognized marriage, determining exactly which years count toward the 10-year marriage-duration threshold described earlier in this chapter can involve some genuine complexity. The SSA has specific guidance for evaluating these situations, generally looking at the date of legal marriage recognition in the relevant jurisdiction at the time. If your situation involves this kind of timeline complexity, it's worth raising it directly and specifically with the SSA, providing whatever documentation you have of the relationship and marriage timeline, rather than assuming ineligibility based on an approximate sense of when the marriage "really" began versus when it was legally documented.

The Emotional Dimension of Reconnecting With an Ex-Spouse's Record

It's worth acknowledging directly that for some readers, the idea of a benefit connected to a former spouse — particularly one from a difficult marriage or divorce — carries emotional weight beyond the financial mechanics described in this chapter. It may help to remember, as covered above, that claiming a divorced-spouse or divorced-survivor benefit involves no direct interaction with your ex-spouse at all: the SSA handles the calculation and payment internally, your ex-spouse is not notified, and your claim has no effect on what they receive. For many people, understanding this administrative separation — that this is a benefit calculated from a record, not a continued relationship or dependency — makes the decision to check eligibility feel more comfortable than it might initially seem.

A Worked Illustration Without Specific Dollar Figures

Consider a hypothetical divorced retiree, Simone, who was married for 16 years before her divorce and has not remarried. Simone's own career, while steady, produced a more modest earnings record than her ex-husband's, whose career included several decades in a higher-paying field. Because her marriage exceeded the 10-year threshold and she remains unmarried, Simone is eligible to have SSA compare her own benefit against a divorced-spouse benefit based on her ex-husband's record, receiving whichever is higher — following exactly the same percentage structure described for current spouses in Chapter Four, simply applied to a marriage that ended in divorce rather than continuing to the present. If Simone's ex-husband later passes away, she would similarly become eligible to have her own benefit compared against a divorced-survivor benefit based on his record, potentially providing a meaningfully larger benefit than either her own record or the divorced-spousal amount would have provided while he was alive, following the same up-to-100%-survivor structure described in Chapter Five.

Divorced-Spouse Benefits and Remarriage Planning

If you're divorced and eligible for a divorced-spouse benefit but are considering remarriage, it's worth understanding clearly how that decision interacts with your eligibility, since the interaction differs depending on which type of benefit is involved. Remarriage generally ends eligibility for a divorced-spousal benefit (the up-to-50% benefit based on a living ex-spouse's record) regardless of your age at remarriage, since that benefit is specifically tied to your current marital status being single. Divorced-survivor benefits, by contrast, follow the same age-60 exception described in Chapter Five for current-spouse survivor benefits — meaning remarriage at 60 or later generally does not end eligibility for a divorced-survivor benefit, even though remarriage at any age would generally end eligibility for a divorced-spousal benefit from a living ex-spouse. If remarriage is on the horizon and either of these benefit types is meaningful to your financial picture, understanding this distinction, and the specific age involved, is worth factoring into your planning and timing conversations.

A Closing Thought on an Underused Benefit Category

Divorced-spouse and divorced-survivor benefits exist because Social Security's designers recognized, decades ago, that a marriage lasting a decade or more often represents a genuine, long-term economic partnership, even if that marriage later ends — and that a spouse who built a life, and sometimes sacrificed career earnings, around that partnership shouldn't lose all connection to the higher earner's Social Security record simply because the marriage ended in divorce rather than death. If this chapter is the first time you're learning that this category of benefit exists, you're not alone — it remains one of the more underutilized provisions in the entire Social Security system, and checking your own eligibility, even on a hunch, costs nothing and can occasionally reveal a benefit meaningfully larger than what you'd assumed you were entitled to based on your own record alone.

A Brief Word on Blended Families

Many households today involve blended families shaped by one or more divorces and remarriages, sometimes with children from multiple relationships. This chapter's rules, combined with the current-spouse rules from

Chapter Four and the survivor rules from Chapter Five, mean that a person's Social Security "family" for benefit purposes can look quite different from their family in an everyday sense — potentially including a current spouse, one or more former spouses from marriages lasting 10 or more years, and dependent children from different relationships, all of whom might have some claim connected to that individual's earnings record, generally without any of these claims reducing what the others receive, as explained throughout this book. If your own family situation is blended in this way, it's genuinely worth a dedicated conversation with the SSA that lays out your full marital and family history, since the various provisions covered in this book interact in ways that are difficult to fully anticipate without walking through your specific timeline with someone who has access to the complete rules.

Keeping Records of Prior Marriages for Future Use

If you anticipate that a divorced-spouse or divorced-survivor benefit might be relevant to your future — even if you're not eligible to claim it for many years — it's worth proactively gathering and safely storing the relevant documentation (marriage certificate, divorce decree, and your ex-spouse's identifying information) now, while it's likely easier to locate than it may be decades from now. Documents from marriages and divorces that occurred long ago can become genuinely difficult to track down as years pass, records offices change their processes, or personal copies are lost in moves or other life transitions. Treating this documentation the way you might treat other important long-term financial records — birth certificates, deeds, or estate planning documents — rather than something to worry about only once you're actually ready to claim, can save meaningful time and frustration when you do eventually need it.

A Quick Reference for This Chapter's Key Numbers

To close this chapter, its central rules are worth summarizing together. The marriage must have lasted at least 10 years, you must currently be unmarried (or, for survivor benefits specifically, remarried at 60 or later), and you must be at least 62 for a divorced-spousal benefit or 60 for a divorced-survivor benefit (50 if disabled). If divorced at least two years, you can generally claim a divorced-spousal benefit even if your ex-spouse hasn't yet filed for their own benefit, unlike the rule for current spouses. Your claim doesn't reduce your ex-spouse's benefit or affect their current spouse's eligibility. And you can hold this same eligibility against more than one former spouse if each marriage met the 10-year threshold, generally receiving whichever produces the higher benefit. These points, held together, are worth checking against your own marital history even if divorce feels like a distant chapter of your life rather than a current financial consideration.

A Final Encouragement to Simply Ask

If there's a single theme running through this chapter, it's that the rules governing divorced-spouse and divorced-survivor benefits are more generous, more private, and more far-reaching than most people assume — and the only real cost of checking your own eligibility is a modest amount of time spent gathering documentation and contacting the SSA. Unlike many financial decisions in this book that involve genuine trade-offs and irreversible consequences, checking your divorced-spouse eligibility carries essentially no downside: at worst, you confirm that your own record already produces the higher benefit, and at best, you uncover a meaningfully larger monthly income you didn't know you were entitled to. Given that asymmetry — modest effort against potentially significant upside — this is one of the lowest-risk, highest-value actions covered anywhere in this book, and it's worth acting on directly rather than setting aside for "someday."

Key Takeaways

If your marriage lasted 10 years or more and you are currently unmarried (or remarried at 60 or later), you may be eligible for benefits based on an ex-spouse's earnings record, following similar percentage rules to current-spouse benefits.

Unlike current-spouse benefits, you can generally claim a divorced-spouse benefit without waiting for your ex-spouse to file, as long as you've been divorced at least two years and your ex-spouse is 62 or older.

Claiming a divorced-spouse or divorced-survivor benefit does not reduce your ex-spouse's own benefit or affect their current spouse's eligibility — each qualifying claim is calculated independently.

These benefits are widely underclaimed simply because people don't realize they still qualify. If you meet the 10-year threshold, check your eligibility with the SSA directly, regardless of how long ago the divorce occurred.

Chapter Seven: How Your Benefits Get Taxed

Many people are surprised to learn that Social Security benefits can be subject to federal income tax — and in some states, state income tax as well. This chapter explains the mechanics of how that taxation works, so you can factor it into your overall retirement income planning rather than being caught off guard.

The Basic Mechanism: Combined Income

Whether your Social Security benefits are taxed, and how much of them are taxed, depends on a measure called "combined income" (sometimes called "provisional income"). Combined income is calculated by adding your adjusted gross income, any tax-exempt interest you received (such as interest from municipal bonds), and half of your Social Security benefits for the year.

That combined income figure is then compared against thresholds that determine what portion of your benefits — if any — becomes subject to federal income tax. Critically, unlike many other parts of the tax code, these thresholds have historically not been adjusted for inflation the way many other tax brackets are, which means that over time, as wages and other income have risen with inflation while the thresholds stayed fixed, a growing share of Social Security recipients have found themselves owing tax on at least part of their benefits. Because this is an area where the underlying law could change, always verify the current thresholds and rules through the IRS or a tax professional rather than relying on any fixed number.

The Two-Tier Structure

The taxation of benefits works in tiers. Below a certain combined income threshold, none of your Social Security benefit is taxable. Above that threshold but below a second, higher threshold, up to 50% of your benefit may become taxable. Above that second, higher threshold, up to 85% of your benefit may become taxable. It's worth being precise about the language here: even at the highest tier, no more than 85% of your Social Security benefit is ever subject to federal income tax — 15% remains untaxed regardless of how high your other income is. This is different from how most other income sources work, and it's a detail worth understanding so you don't overestimate your tax exposure.

The specific dollar thresholds differ depending on your filing status — generally lower thresholds for single filers and higher thresholds for married couples filing jointly, though notably not simply double the single-filer thresholds. Married couples filing separately, particularly those who lived with their spouse at any point during the year, often face especially unfavorable treatment under these rules, generally with little or no tax-free threshold at all — this is a detail worth flagging to a tax professional specifically if that filing status applies to you.

Why This Catches People Off Guard

A common pattern: someone retires, expects that because they're no longer earning a "paycheck," Social Security will be their tax-free reward for decades of contributions. Then tax season arrives, and they discover that between their Social Security benefit, a pension, required minimum distributions from retirement accounts, and any part-time work or investment income, their combined income pushes a meaningful share of their Social Security benefit into taxable territory.

This isn't a flaw in your planning — it's simply how the system is structured, and it becomes more relevant the more diversified and successful your other retirement income sources are. Higher-income retirees, precisely because they've built other resources, are more likely to see a larger share of their Social Security benefits taxed. Understanding this in advance allows you to plan around it, rather than being surprised by it.

Planning Angles Worth Discussing With a Tax Professional

While this book does not offer personalized tax advice, there are a few general planning concepts worth being aware of, so you know what questions to bring to a professional:

The order and timing of withdrawals from different account types (taxable brokerage accounts, tax-deferred accounts like traditional IRAs and 401(k)s, and tax-free accounts like Roth IRAs) can influence your combined income in a given year, and therefore how much of your

Social Security benefit becomes taxable in that year. Coordinating withdrawal strategy across account types, ideally with professional guidance, can sometimes reduce the overall tax burden compared to an uncoordinated approach.

Required minimum distributions (RMDs) from certain retirement accounts, which generally must begin at an age set by current law, are not optional and will factor into your combined income whether or not you need the cash. Some people proactively convert portions of tax-deferred accounts to Roth accounts in years before RMDs begin, specifically to reduce future RMD-driven combined income — this is a strategy with its own trade-offs and should be evaluated with a tax professional, not adopted casually.

The timing of when you claim Social Security itself interacts with this chapter's topic too: because combined income includes half of whatever Social Security benefit you're receiving, claiming a larger benefit (through delayed claiming) does modestly raise the amount of your benefit that's included in the combined income calculation — though this is generally a secondary consideration compared to the claiming-age factors covered in Chapters Two and Three.

State Taxes Vary Widely

Federal taxation of Social Security benefits, as described above, applies uniformly based on federal law, but state-level treatment varies enormously. As of recent years, the substantial majority of states do not tax Social Security benefits at all, while a smaller number of states do tax them, sometimes with their own separate income thresholds or exemptions that differ from the federal rules. Because state tax policy changes periodically and differs so much from state to state, check your specific state's current treatment directly — through your state's department of revenue or a tax professional familiar with your state — rather than assuming based on general reputation or outdated information.

An Illustration

Consider a hypothetical retired couple, Wendell and Carol, filing jointly. Between Wendell's Social Security benefit, Carol's smaller spousal benefit, a modest pension Wendell receives, and required distributions from a 401(k) they built over their careers, their combined income for the year lands solidly above the higher threshold for joint filers. As a result, up to 85% of their combined Social Security benefits may be included in their taxable income for the year — not 85% of their total income, but up to 85% of the Social Security portion specifically, taxed at their normal marginal tax rate alongside their other income.

This doesn't mean Wendell and Carol made a mistake by building other retirement resources — quite the opposite, it generally means their overall retirement income picture is stronger than it would be relying on Social Security alone. It simply means their tax picture in retirement is more complex than "Social Security is tax-free," and working with a tax professional to manage withdrawal timing across their different accounts is a worthwhile investment for a couple in their position.

Walking Through the Combined Income Test Step by Step

Because the combined income calculation described earlier in this chapter can feel abstract, it may help to walk through the general steps conceptually, without attaching specific dollar figures that would quickly become outdated.

First, start with your adjusted gross income for the year — generally your total income from wages (if any), pensions, retirement account withdrawals, investment income, and similar sources, after certain adjustments, but before subtracting your standard or itemized deductions. Second, add any tax-exempt interest you received, most commonly from municipal bonds — this is income the IRS doesn't tax directly, but it still counts toward this specific combined income calculation. Third, add exactly half of the Social Security benefits you received during the year — not your full benefit amount, just half of it.

The sum of those three figures is your combined income for the purposes of this test. That figure is then compared against your filing status's specific thresholds to determine whether 0%, up to 50%, or up to 85% of your Social Security benefit gets added to your taxable income for the year, following the tiered structure described earlier in this chapter. Once you know which tier applies, the specific taxable portion of your benefit is calculated using a formula the IRS provides (often through a worksheet in the Form 1040 instructions, or automatically by tax preparation software), which determines the exact taxable amount within that tier — it isn't simply "all or nothing" at each threshold, but a more gradual calculation within each tier.

Voluntary Tax Withholding on Social Security Benefits

Many retirees are surprised to learn that Social Security benefits are not automatically subject to income tax withholding the way a paycheck typically is. If part of your benefit is taxable, as described above, and you don't arrange for any withholding, you may owe a potentially significant amount when you file your tax return, which can be an unwelcome surprise if you haven't planned for it, or in some cases can trigger an underpayment penalty if the amount owed is large enough.

Fortunately, the SSA offers voluntary tax withholding on benefits, generally through a form called the W-4V, which allows you to choose to have a flat percentage of your monthly benefit withheld and sent to the IRS on your behalf, similar in spirit to how withholding works from a paycheck. This isn't required, but for retirees who know a portion of their benefit is likely to be taxable, opting into voluntary withholding — or alternatively, making quarterly estimated tax payments directly to the IRS — is a common and sensible way to avoid an unpleasant surprise at tax time. A tax professional can help you estimate an appropriate withholding percentage based on your full income picture.

Common Tax Mistakes Retirees Make

One common mistake is assuming, incorrectly, that because Social Security is "your money" coming back to you, it must be tax-free — as this chapter has explained, that's often not the case once other income enters the picture. A second common mistake is failing to anticipate how a large one-time event — selling a home, a large capital gain, a big Roth conversion, or a large retirement account withdrawal — can spike your combined income for that specific year, pushing more of your Social Security benefit into taxable territory for that year specifically, even if your income is more modest in surrounding years. Because this chapter's thresholds apply on a year-by-year basis, planning around when large one-time income events occur — spreading them across multiple years where possible, for instance — can sometimes meaningfully reduce the total tax impact, though this requires the kind of detailed modeling a tax professional is best positioned to do.

A third mistake is overlooking the state tax dimension entirely, assuming that because most states don't tax Social Security benefits, no state does — as covered below, a minority of states do, and if you live in (or are considering relocating to) one of them, it's worth factoring into your overall retirement income and location planning.

State Tax Treatment in More Depth

As mentioned earlier in this chapter, most states do not tax Social Security benefits at all, and among the smaller number that do, several offer their own exemptions or income thresholds below which benefits still escape state taxation, meaning even residents of a "taxing" state may end up owing little or nothing depending on their specific income level. Because state legislatures periodically revisit this policy — some states have moved toward eliminating Social Security taxation in recent years — the list of which states tax benefits and under what conditions is genuinely a moving target, not a fixed piece of trivia. If state taxation of your benefits is a meaningful factor in your retirement location planning, verify the current policy for any state you're considering directly through that state's department of revenue, rather than relying on outdated lists that may circulate online or in older publications.

Lump-Sum and Retroactive Payments

Occasionally, a retiree receives a retroactive lump-sum payment from Social Security — for instance, if there was a delay in processing a claim, or if you claimed benefits with an effective date somewhat earlier than your actual application date, within the retroactive limits the SSA allows for retirement claims made after FRA. Receiving a large lump sum in a single tax year can push that year's combined income substantially higher than a typical year, potentially pushing more of that year's Social

Security income into taxable territory than would have applied had the same total been received in smaller amounts spread across multiple years.

Helpfully, the tax code includes a specific provision allowing recipients of a lump-sum Social Security payment that includes benefits attributable to an earlier year to elect to calculate the tax as if the payment had been received in the years it was actually attributable to, if that produces a better result than including it all in the year received. This calculation is detailed enough that it's generally best handled by a tax professional or tax software specifically designed to account for it, but it's worth being aware that this option exists if you ever receive a substantial retroactive or lump-sum Social Security payment, rather than assuming you're stuck with the full tax impact falling in a single year.

Charitable Giving as a Combined-Income Management Tool

For retirees who are charitably inclined and who take required minimum distributions from a traditional IRA, a qualified charitable distribution (QCD) is worth understanding as a tool that connects directly to this chapter's topic. A QCD allows an eligible IRA owner (generally starting at a specific age set by current law) to direct a distribution straight to a qualifying charity, where that amount generally is not included in adjusted gross income at all — unlike a standard withdrawal followed by a separate charitable donation, which does count as income before any charitable deduction is applied.

Because a QCD keeps the distributed amount out of adjusted gross income entirely, it can help keep combined income (described earlier in this chapter) lower than it would otherwise be, which can, in turn, help keep more of your Social Security benefit outside the taxable tiers, and can also help manage IRMAA thresholds discussed in Chapter Nine. This is a strategy worth discussing with a tax professional if charitable giving is already part of your retirement plan, since the potential double benefit — supporting a cause you care about while managing taxable income — is one of the more elegant intersections between tax planning and personal values available to retirees with IRA assets.

A Second Illustration: A Retiree With Rental Income

Consider a hypothetical retiree, Antoine, who owns a rental property generating steady income alongside his Social Security benefit and a modest pension. Rental income, after allowable expenses and depreciation, generally counts toward adjusted gross income and therefore toward the combined income calculation described earlier in this chapter, even though it isn't "earned income" in the sense relevant to the retirement earnings test covered in Chapter Two (which applies specifically to wages and self-employment income, not passive rental income, for someone claiming benefits before FRA).

Because Antoine's rental income is a relatively steady, predictable addition to his combined income each year, he's in a good position to work with a tax professional to project his combined income in advance and understand which tier of Social Security taxation he's likely to fall into most years, allowing him to plan his voluntary tax withholding (described earlier in this chapter) accordingly, rather than being surprised by his tax liability each spring.

How This Chapter Connects to Your Claiming-Age Decision

It's worth closing this chapter by tying its topic back to the claiming-age decision covered in Chapters Two and Three, since taxation is one of the factors that can meaningfully influence, though rarely single-handedly determine, that earlier decision. A larger benefit obtained through delayed claiming means a larger amount potentially subject to taxation in retirement, but it's important to keep this in perspective: even in the highest tier described earlier in this chapter, no more than 85% of your benefit is ever taxed, meaning a larger benefit before tax is still, after tax, larger than a smaller benefit would have been — the tax impact reduces the advantage of delaying somewhat, but does not eliminate it or reverse the underlying math. This is a secondary consideration worth being aware of, not a reason to abandon delayed claiming if the other factors from Chapters Two and Three point in that direction for your household.

Working With a Tax Professional on This Specific Topic

If you don't currently work with a tax professional but are approaching retirement, this chapter's topics — combined income thresholds, RMD and Roth conversion timing, voluntary withholding, and state tax variation — are collectively a reasonable trigger point for engaging one, even if only for a single planning session focused specifically on your retirement income tax picture rather than ongoing annual tax preparation. Many tax professionals offer retirement-transition planning as a discrete service, and the potential tax savings from coordinated withdrawal timing across a multi-decade retirement can meaningfully exceed the cost of that planning session, particularly for households with multiple income sources feeding into the combined income calculation described throughout this chapter.

A Brief Recap of the Combined Income Test in Plain Terms

Given how much ground this chapter has covered, it may help to restate the core idea one final time in the simplest possible terms: the more total income your household has from all sources combined — including half of your Social Security benefit itself — the more likely it is that a portion of your Social Security benefit becomes taxable, up to a ceiling of 85% of the benefit. This is a gradual, tiered system rather than an all-or-nothing cliff, filing status changes the specific thresholds involved, and the underlying dollar thresholds are not adjusted for inflation the way many other parts of the tax code are, meaning more retirees have gradually become subject to this taxation over time as incomes have risen. Keeping this core idea in mind, even without memorizing every specific rule covered in this chapter, will serve you well as you plan your retirement income strategy alongside a tax professional.

A Note on Tax Software and Its Limitations Here

Many retirees prepare their own taxes using consumer tax software, which generally handles the combined income calculation and the taxable-benefit worksheet described in this chapter automatically and accurately once you've entered your income information correctly. Where tax software is less helpful is in the proactive planning side of this chapter's topics — deciding how to time a Roth conversion, whether to use a qualified charitable distribution, or how to sequence withdrawals across account types to manage your combined income across multiple future years. Software is generally built to calculate the tax consequences of decisions you've already made for a given year, not to model multi-year strategies across different possible choices. If your situation is simple, software alone may be sufficient; if you're weighing meaningful strategic decisions with multi-year consequences, that's where a human tax professional's forward-looking planning adds value software alone typically doesn't provide.

A Quick Reference for This Chapter's Key Numbers

To close this chapter, its central mechanics are worth restating together one final time. Combined income equals your adjusted gross income, plus tax-exempt interest, plus half of your Social Security benefit. Below a lower threshold, none of your benefit is taxable; between the lower and a higher threshold, up to 50% may be taxable; above the higher threshold, up to 85% may be taxable — but never more than 85%, regardless of how high your other income is. Thresholds differ by filing status and have not historically been adjusted for inflation. And most states don't tax Social Security benefits at all, though a minority do, with rules that vary and change. These mechanics, more than any specific dollar figure, are what will still be useful to you years from now when you sit down with a tax professional to apply them to your own current numbers.

Key Takeaways

Whether your Social Security benefits are taxed depends on "combined income" — your adjusted gross income, tax-exempt interest, and half of your Social Security benefit — compared against thresholds that differ by filing status.

Depending on your combined income, 0%, up to 50%, or up to 85% of your benefit may be included in your taxable income — but no more than 85% is ever taxed, regardless of how high your other income is.

Coordinating withdrawals across taxable, tax-deferred, and tax-free accounts, and planning for required minimum distributions in advance, can meaningfully affect how much of your Social Security benefit ends up taxed — this is a strong area for professional tax guidance.

Most states do not tax Social Security benefits, but a minority do, with rules that vary and change — verify your specific state's current treatment rather than relying on general assumptions.

Chapter Eight: Medicare Timing and Avoiding Costly Penalties

Medicare and Social Security are administered separately, but for most people approaching retirement, they arrive on nearly the same timeline, and the decisions around each affect the other. Medicare enrollment timing, in particular, comes with penalty structures that are permanent — not one-time fees, but lifetime surcharges added to your premiums for as long as you're enrolled. This chapter walks through the enrollment windows and the penalties for missing them, so you can plan ahead rather than discover the rules after it's too late to avoid a penalty.

The Basic Structure of Medicare

Medicare is generally composed of several parts. Part A covers hospital insurance and is premium-free for most people who paid Medicare payroll taxes for enough years during their working life. Part B covers medical insurance — outpatient care, doctor visits, and similar services — and generally requires a monthly premium regardless of work history. Part D covers prescription drug coverage, offered through private plans that follow Medicare's rules, and also generally involves a monthly premium. Many people also choose a Medicare Advantage plan (Part C), which bundles Parts A and B (and often D) through a private insurer, as an alternative to Original Medicare, or a Medigap supplemental policy to help cover costs Original Medicare doesn't.

This book focuses on enrollment timing, since that's where the highest-stakes, hardest-to-reverse decisions live — the specific choice between Original Medicare and Medicare Advantage, or which supplemental policy to choose, is a more personal decision best discussed with a Medicare counselor or advisor familiar with your health needs and location.

The Initial Enrollment Period

Your Initial Enrollment Period (IEP) is a seven-month window centered on your 65th birthday: it begins three months before the month you turn 65, includes your birthday month itself, and extends three months after. This is the primary window most people use to enroll in Medicare Parts A and B, and it is worth marking clearly on a calendar well in advance, because missing it without a valid exception can trigger penalties that follow you for the rest of your life.

If you are already receiving Social Security retirement benefits when you turn 65, you are generally automatically enrolled in Medicare Parts A and B without needing to actively apply — you'll simply receive your Medicare card in the mail. If you have not yet claimed Social Security by 65 (which, based on the earlier chapters of this book, may well be your situation if you're planning to delay claiming past 65), you generally need to actively enroll in Medicare yourself during your IEP — Medicare eligibility and Social Security claiming are not the same decision, and delaying one does not automatically delay the other.

This is one of the most important practical takeaways in this entire book: if you plan to delay claiming Social Security past 65, as discussed in Chapters Two and Three, you still generally need to actively sign up for Medicare around your 65th birthday, separately, or risk a penalty for late enrollment. Do not assume the two are linked.

The Part B Late Enrollment Penalty

If you don't sign up for Part B when you're first eligible, and you don't qualify for a valid exception (covered below), you may face a late enrollment penalty: your Part B premium may increase by a percentage for each 12-month period you were eligible but not enrolled, and this penalty generally applies for as long as you have Part B — it is not temporary. Because this penalty compounds with each full 12-month period of delay and lasts indefinitely, understanding your enrollment window in advance is far more valuable than trying to fix a missed window after the fact.

The Part D Late Enrollment Penalty

A similar, separately calculated late enrollment penalty applies to Part D prescription drug coverage if you go without "creditable" drug coverage (coverage at least as good as Medicare's standard) for 63 or more consecutive days after your Initial Enrollment Period ends. Like the Part B penalty, this one also generally lasts for as long as you have Part D coverage, accumulating based on the length of the gap.

The Key Exception: Employer Coverage

The most common and important exception to these enrollment windows applies to people who are still covered by a group health plan through their own or a spouse's active employment at a company with a sufficient number of employees (a threshold that determines whether the employer plan or Medicare is considered "primary" — worth confirming the current employee-count threshold with Medicare or your employer's benefits department). In that situation, you may be able to delay Medicare enrollment past 65 without penalty, and instead enroll later during a Special Enrollment Period, generally available for a period after the employer coverage or the employment itself ends.

This exception is genuinely valuable for people who plan to work past 65 with solid employer coverage, but it comes with an important caveat: it generally applies to larger-employer group coverage specifically, not to all forms of health coverage. COBRA continuation coverage and retiree health plans, for example, generally do not count as active employment coverage for this purpose, and relying on them past your IEP without also enrolling in Medicare can trigger the very penalties this exception is meant to help you avoid. If you are planning to work past 65 and want to delay Medicare, confirm directly with your employer's benefits administrator and with Medicare that your specific coverage qualifies for the Special Enrollment Period exception before you rely on it.

Health Savings Accounts and Medicare

If you or your employer have been contributing to a Health Savings Account (HSA) alongside a high-deductible health plan, enrolling in any part of Medicare (including the Part A that many people get automatically) generally makes you ineligible to continue contributing to an HSA going forward. Some people specifically choose to delay all Medicare enrollment, including Part A, for this reason, if they're still working and want to keep contributing to an HSA. This is a nuanced, individual decision — HSAs offer valuable tax advantages, but delaying Medicare has its own trade-offs — and it's worth discussing with a benefits advisor if it applies to you.

Also worth noting: enrolling in Social Security retirement benefits at or after 65 generally triggers automatic Part A enrollment (since Part A is premium-free for most people), which in turn can end HSA eligibility even if you didn't proactively choose Part A. If you're planning to delay Social Security specifically to preserve HSA contributions, make sure that plan accounts for this automatic-enrollment interaction.

An Illustration

Consider a hypothetical worker, Fatima, who plans to continue working full-time past 65 at a mid-sized company with a solid employer health plan, and who plans to delay claiming Social Security until 70 as discussed in Chapter Two. Fatima's employer coverage likely qualifies her for the Special Enrollment Period exception, meaning she may be able to delay Medicare Part B enrollment without penalty until she actually stops working or loses that coverage. However, because she has not claimed Social Security, she will not be automatically enrolled in Medicare Part A at 65 — if she wants Part A coverage (which is premium-free for her and can serve as secondary coverage alongside her employer plan), she generally needs to actively apply for it, even while delaying Part B.

Contrast this with a hypothetical retiree, Oswald, who plans to fully retire at 65 with no employer coverage waiting in the wings. Oswald has no exception available and needs to actively enroll in Medicare Parts A and B (and likely Part D, or a Medicare Advantage plan that includes drug coverage) during his Initial Enrollment Period, regardless of whether he is claiming Social Security at that time, in order to avoid the late enrollment penalties described above.

Original Medicare Versus Medicare Advantage: A Timing Note

While the detailed comparison between Original Medicare (Parts A and B, often paired with a separate Part D plan and sometimes a Medigap supplemental policy) and Medicare Advantage (Part C, which bundles coverage through a private insurer) is a personal decision that depends heavily on your health needs, preferred doctors and hospitals, and location, there is one timing-related point worth flagging here. Your Initial Enrollment Period is generally the most favorable time to make this choice, particularly if you're interested in a Medigap supplemental policy alongside Original Medicare: during a specific window tied to your Part B enrollment, you generally have a right to purchase a Medigap policy without medical underwriting, meaning an insurer generally cannot deny you coverage or charge you more based on health conditions during that window. Outside that window, in many states, Medigap insurers can medically underwrite applicants, potentially making a policy more expensive or harder to obtain later if your health has changed.

This is a meaningful reason to think through your Original Medicare versus Medicare Advantage decision carefully around your Initial Enrollment Period, rather than treating it as a choice you can costlessly revisit at any point later — while there are annual opportunities to change plans, the specific medical-underwriting protection for Medigap policies is generally tied to that initial window, and switching from Medicare Advantage back to Original Medicare with a Medigap policy later in life can, in some states, involve medical underwriting that didn't apply the first time around.

Special Enrollment Periods Beyond Employer Coverage

The employer-coverage exception described earlier in this chapter is the most common Special Enrollment Period, but it isn't the only circumstance that can allow enrollment or plan changes outside the standard windows. Other situations — such as moving outside your current plan's service area, losing other creditable coverage unexpectedly, or certain plan-specific changes — can also trigger Special Enrollment Periods with their own specific rules and timeframes. If you find yourself in a life circumstance that doesn't fit neatly into the standard Initial Enrollment Period or the employer-coverage exception, it's worth checking directly with Medicare (through medicare.gov or by phone) about whether a Special Enrollment Period might apply to your specific situation, rather than assuming you've missed your window entirely.

The COBRA and Retiree Coverage Trap, Explained Further

This point is important enough to restate with more detail, because it's one of the costliest and most common Medicare timing mistakes. When employment ends — whether through retirement, layoff, or another reason — many people are offered COBRA continuation coverage, which allows them to remain on their former employer's health plan for a limited period, generally by paying the full premium themselves. Separately, some retirees are offered a retiree health plan by a former employer, which continues some form of coverage into retirement.

Neither COBRA coverage nor a retiree health plan generally counts as "active employment" coverage for purposes of the Medicare Special Enrollment Period exception described earlier in this chapter. This means that if you leave active employment at or after 65, your Initial Enrollment Period (or the

Special Enrollment Period tied to the end of your active employment, if you delayed Medicare while still actively working) generally begins running at that point, regardless of whether you then transition onto COBRA or a retiree plan. People sometimes assume that because they still have "coverage" through COBRA or a retiree plan, they've satisfied their Medicare enrollment obligation — they haven't, and the late enrollment penalty clock for Part B and Part D can be running in the background even while COBRA or retiree coverage is active. If you're transitioning off active employment coverage into COBRA or a retiree plan at or after 65, treat that transition as your cue to enroll in Medicare promptly, not as a reason to wait further.

A Practical Medicare Enrollment Checklist

Given how many moving pieces this chapter covers, it may help to have a simple checklist to work through as you approach 65, or as you approach the end of active employment if that happens at a different time. Confirm whether you'll be automatically enrolled (generally the case if you're already receiving Social Security) or need to actively apply. If you're still working, confirm with your employer's benefits department whether your specific coverage qualifies for the Special Enrollment Period exception, and get that confirmation in writing if possible. Mark your Initial Enrollment Period dates clearly, remembering it's a seven-month window centered on your 65th birthday month. Decide, ideally with the help of a Medicare counselor or advisor, between Original

Medicare (with or without a Medigap policy and a separate Part D plan) and Medicare Advantage, keeping the medical-underwriting timing note above in mind. And if you have an HSA, revisit the interaction between Medicare enrollment and HSA eligibility described earlier in this chapter before finalizing your timing.

Medicare Savings Programs and Extra Help for Lower-Income Beneficiaries

Not every aspect of Medicare timing and cost involves higher-income considerations like IRMAA, covered in the next chapter. For beneficiaries with more limited income and resources, several programs exist to help cover Medicare costs — broadly referred to as Medicare Savings Programs, which can help pay Part B premiums and, depending on the specific program, other cost-sharing amounts, along with a separate program commonly called "Extra Help," which assists with Part D prescription drug plan costs for qualifying lower-income beneficiaries.

Eligibility for these programs generally depends on income and resource limits that are updated periodically and vary somewhat by state for the Medicare Savings Programs specifically, since they're administered in coordination with each state's Medicaid agency. If your household income is more limited, or you're helping a family member navigate Medicare on a limited income, it's worth checking eligibility for these programs directly through your state Medicaid office or through the Social Security Administration for

Extra Help specifically, since they can meaningfully reduce the out-of-pocket cost of Medicare coverage for those who qualify, and many eligible people don't realize these programs exist.

Traveling Abroad and Medicare's Limitations

A detail that surprises many retirees who plan to travel or live part-time outside the United States: Original Medicare generally does not cover healthcare services received outside the United States, with only narrow exceptions. Some Medicare Advantage plans and some Medigap supplemental policies offer limited foreign travel emergency coverage, but this varies significantly by specific plan, so it's not something to assume you have without checking your specific policy's terms directly.

If extended travel or part-time residency abroad is part of your retirement plans, this is worth researching specifically — whether through supplemental travel medical insurance, a Medigap policy with foreign travel benefits, or simply understanding and budgeting for the gap in coverage — well before you need it, rather than discovering the limitation during a medical emergency in another country.

A Brief Note on Long-Term Care

It's worth being clear about something Medicare does not do, since the confusion is common and the financial stakes of misunderstanding it are high: Medicare generally does not cover long-term custodial care — the kind of extended assistance with daily living activities provided in many nursing homes or by long-term home health aides — beyond limited, short-term skilled nursing coverage following a qualifying hospital stay. Long-term custodial care is a substantial, often underappreciated retirement planning gap that Medicare simply isn't designed to fill, and it's a topic that deserves its own dedicated research and planning conversation with a financial advisor, separate from the Medicare enrollment timing topics covered in this chapter — ideally well before care needs become urgent, since planning options (including long-term care insurance) are generally more available and more affordable earlier in retirement, or even before retirement, than after a health need has already emerged.

Coordinating Medicare Timing With Your Spouse

If you're married, it's worth remembering that Medicare eligibility and enrollment timing are determined individually, based on each spouse's own age, rather than as a household unit the way some Social Security benefits are. This means spouses with different ages will generally reach their own Initial Enrollment Periods at different times, and each spouse needs to navigate their own enrollment decisions and potential employer-coverage exceptions independently, even if they're currently covered under the same employer health plan. A common scenario worth planning for explicitly: if a working spouse's employer plan covers both spouses, and the working spouse is younger than the Medicare-eligible spouse, the older spouse may need to transition onto Medicare at 65 even while the younger spouse continues on the employer plan — meaning the household may end up managing two different types of coverage simultaneously for a period, which is worth anticipating rather than discovering at the last minute.

A Brief Summary of the Medicare Timing Mistakes This Chapter Aims to Prevent

Given how many specific rules this chapter has covered, it may help to name the core mistakes one more time, clearly, as a closing summary: missing your Initial Enrollment Period without a valid employer-coverage exception, resulting in permanent late-enrollment penalties; assuming COBRA or retiree coverage qualifies as active employment coverage when it generally does not; assuming that delaying Social Security claiming automatically delays your Medicare obligations, when the two systems run independently; and overlooking the Medigap medical-underwriting timing window described earlier in this chapter if a Medigap policy is part of your plan. Avoiding these specific, well-defined mistakes goes a long way toward a smooth Medicare transition, even without mastering every detail of the broader Medicare system.

Where to Get Unbiased Medicare Guidance

Because Medicare involves private insurance products layered on top of a federal program, it's worth knowing where to find guidance that isn't tied to selling you a specific plan. Every state has a free State Health Insurance Assistance Program (commonly known by an acronym like SHIP, though the exact local name varies), staffed largely by trained counselors and volunteers who provide one-on-one Medicare guidance without any connection to insurance sales commissions. This is generally a more neutral starting point than a conversation with an insurance agent who earns a commission on the specific plan they recommend, particularly for the foundational timing and enrollment questions covered in this chapter. Medicare.gov and the official Medicare helpline are similarly neutral, official sources for enrollment rules and deadlines. Once you've used these resources to understand your options and timing, engaging with a licensed insurance agent to compare specific plan offerings is a reasonable next step — just with a clearer sense already in hand of what you're actually looking for.

A Quick Reference for This Chapter's Key Numbers

To close this chapter, its essential timing rules are worth restating together. Your Initial Enrollment Period is a seven-month window centered on your 65th birthday month — three months before, the birthday month itself, and three months after. Missing it without a valid exception can trigger Part B and Part D late-enrollment penalties that generally last for as long as you carry that coverage. Active employer group coverage through your own or a spouse's current employment (not COBRA, not retiree coverage) is the main valid reason to delay without penalty, using a Special Enrollment Period later. And Medicare enrollment obligations run independently of your Social Security claiming timeline — delaying one does not delay the other. These four points are the backbone of avoiding the costly, permanent mistakes this chapter has been devoted to helping you sidestep.

Key Takeaways

Your Initial Enrollment Period for Medicare is a seven-month window centered on your 65th birthday, and missing it without a valid exception can trigger Part B and Part D late enrollment penalties that generally last for as long as you carry that coverage.

Delaying Social Security claiming (as discussed in Chapters Two and Three) does not delay your Medicare enrollment obligations — the two are separate systems, and you generally need to actively enroll in Medicare around 65 even if you haven't claimed Social Security yet.

Active employer group health coverage (through your own or a spouse's current employment at a qualifying employer) is the main valid reason to delay Medicare Part B without penalty, using a Special Enrollment Period later — but COBRA and retiree coverage generally do not qualify for this exception.

If you rely on a Health Savings Account, understand that enrolling in any part of Medicare, including automatic Part A enrollment triggered by claiming Social Security, generally ends your ability to contribute to that HSA going forward.

Chapter Nine: Understanding IRMAA and Income-Related Surcharges

Once you understand Medicare's basic enrollment structure, there's one more piece worth understanding clearly, because it surprises higher-income retirees more than almost any other rule in this book: the Income-Related Monthly Adjustment Amount, or IRMAA. This chapter explains what it is, how it's calculated, and what to do if your income changes in a way that should affect it.

What IRMAA Is

IRMAA is a surcharge added to the standard Medicare Part B premium, and separately to Part D premiums, for people whose income exceeds certain thresholds. It is not a penalty for late enrollment (that's the separate mechanism covered in the previous chapter) — it is simply a higher premium tier for higher-income beneficiaries, similar in spirit to a progressive tax bracket, though it is technically a premium adjustment administered by Social Security rather than a tax administered by the IRS.

How Income Is Measured

IRMAA is based on your Modified Adjusted Gross Income (MAGI) — generally your adjusted gross income plus tax-exempt interest — as reported on your tax return. Critically, IRMAA determinations generally use your tax return from two years prior to the current year, because that's the most recent complete tax data available to the Social Security Administration when premiums are set for a given year. This two-year lookback is one of the most important mechanical details to understand, because it means your Medicare premiums this year may be based on an income level from a period in your life that no longer reflects your current situation — for example, your last full year of high earnings before retirement, even though you've since stopped working and your income has dropped substantially.

The Tiered Structure

IRMAA works in income brackets — as your MAGI from two years prior rises past each threshold, you move into a higher premium tier for both Part B and Part D, with the surcharge amount increasing at each tier. There are multiple tiers, and the specific dollar thresholds and corresponding surcharge amounts are adjusted periodically (generally annually), so this is very much an area where you need to check the current-year figures at ssa.gov or medicare.gov rather than relying on any number written in a book — a threshold that seems high today may feel quite different after a few years of inflation and periodic adjustment.

The "Life-Changing Event" Appeal

This is, in many ways, the single most valuable piece of information in this chapter, and it's something many people simply never learn about: if your income has dropped significantly since the tax year used for your current IRMAA determination — due to a specific, defined "life-changing event" — you can request that the SSA use more current income information instead of the two-year-old tax return data.

Qualifying life-changing events generally include retirement or reduction in work hours, marriage, divorce or annulment, death of a spouse, loss of income-producing property due to a disaster or other circumstances beyond your control, loss or reduction of certain pension income, and an employer settlement payment related to the employer's closure or bankruptcy. This is generally requested using a specific SSA form (commonly referenced as Form SSA-44), where you report the life-changing event and provide updated income evidence.

This appeal mechanism exists precisely for the common situation described above: someone whose income was high in their last working year or two, triggering IRMAA surcharges, whose income has since dropped meaningfully in retirement. Without filing this appeal, you could end up paying elevated Medicare premiums for a year or two longer than your actual current income would otherwise require, simply because the standard lookback period hasn't caught up to your new, lower income yet.

What Doesn't Qualify

It's worth being clear about what generally does not count as a qualifying life-changing event for this appeal: a general decline in the stock market reducing your investment account values, for instance, generally is not itself a qualifying event, even though it affects your finances. The list of qualifying events is specific and somewhat narrow, focused on discrete life changes rather than general income or asset fluctuations. If you're unsure whether your situation qualifies, it's worth asking the SSA directly rather than assuming either way.

IRMAA and the Claiming and Tax Planning Chapters

IRMAA connects directly to concepts from earlier chapters. Because IRMAA is based on MAGI, and because required minimum distributions, Roth conversions, and other income-timing decisions discussed in Chapter Seven all affect MAGI, decisions made purely for income-tax reasons can inadvertently push you into a higher IRMAA bracket two years later, adding a Medicare premium surcharge on top of whatever income tax consequences were already being weighed. This is a strong argument for coordinating your broader retirement income and tax planning — including any large one-time income events, such as a Roth conversion or the sale of an asset with a large capital gain — with an eye toward IRMAA thresholds specifically, not just income tax brackets, ideally with the help of a financial or tax advisor who considers both together.

An Illustration

Consider a hypothetical retiree, Gerald, who earned a high salary in his final two years of full-time work, then retired completely, living afterward primarily on Social Security and modest investment income at a much lower total level. Because IRMAA determinations for a given year generally rely on tax data from two years prior, Gerald may find himself paying elevated, higher-tier Medicare premiums in his first year or two of retirement — based on the high income from his last working years — even though his actual current income no longer supports that tier. By proactively filing a life-changing-event appeal with the SSA, reporting his retirement and providing evidence of his new, lower income level, Gerald may be able to have his premiums recalculated based on his current circumstances rather than waiting for the standard two-year lookback to naturally catch up.

Filing the Life-Changing Event Appeal, Step by Step

If you believe a qualifying life-changing event applies to your situation, the general process involves obtaining and completing the relevant SSA form (commonly Form SSA-44), which asks you to identify which specific life-changing event applies from the qualifying list, and to provide evidence supporting your claim of reduced income — this might include a signed statement, a more recent tax return if one is available, or other documentation depending on the nature of the event. You can generally submit this form by mail or in person at a local SSA field office, and in some cases discuss your situation by phone first to confirm which documentation will be needed for your specific circumstance.

It's worth being reasonably prompt about this once you're aware a qualifying event has occurred, since the recalculation generally applies going forward from when it's processed, rather than being automatically backdated indefinitely — though specific retroactivity rules can apply depending on the circumstances, which is worth clarifying directly with the SSA representative handling your case.

Why IRMAA Brackets Are Sometimes Called "Cliffs"

One detail about IRMAA that catches people off guard, and that's worth understanding clearly, is that the bracket structure can behave like a "cliff" rather than a smooth gradient in certain cases — meaning that crossing a threshold by even a small amount can move your entire premium into the next tier, rather than only the income above the threshold being subject to the higher rate the way many people assume income tax brackets work (and even income tax brackets, contrary to common belief, only tax the amount within each bracket, not your entire income at the top bracket rate — but IRMAA's structure has historically worked differently, applying the higher premium tier to the whole benefit once you cross a threshold).

This is exactly why the topics in this chapter connect so directly to the tax-planning concepts in Chapter Seven: a Roth conversion or a large one-time withdrawal that pushes your MAGI just over an IRMAA threshold in a given year (remembering the two-year lookback) can result in a premium increase disproportionate to how far over the threshold your income actually landed. Because of this "cliff" effect, it's often worth specifically checking, when planning any large one-time income event, exactly where the nearest IRMAA threshold sits relative to your projected income for that year, and whether staying just under it is feasible — this is a detail-oriented calculation well suited to a tax or financial professional with access to the current-year threshold figures.

Appealing an IRMAA Determination You Believe Is Incorrect

Separate from the life-changing-event process described above (which addresses a genuine change in your circumstances), there's also a distinct process for disputing an IRMAA determination you believe is factually incorrect — for instance, if the tax return data the SSA used doesn't match what you actually filed, due to an amended return, a filing error, or a data transmission issue between the IRS and SSA. In that situation, the appropriate path is generally a formal appeal or reconsideration request, rather than the life-changing-event form, since you're disputing the accuracy of the underlying data rather than reporting a change in circumstances. If you receive an IRMAA determination that doesn't match your understanding of your own tax return, it's worth contacting the SSA promptly to clarify which process — the life-changing-event appeal or a data-accuracy dispute — fits your specific situation.

A Second Illustration: A Couple Navigating a Retirement Transition

Consider a hypothetical couple, Alden and Ruth, both retiring within the same year after decades of solid dual-career income. Their MAGI from two years prior — reflecting their last full year of working income — places them well into one of the higher IRMAA tiers for both Part B and Part D. In their first year or two of retirement, before their lower post-retirement income has had time to work its way through the standard two-year lookback, they may be paying premiums calculated on income they no longer earn.

Because "retirement" is explicitly one of the qualifying life-changing events described earlier in this chapter, Alden and Ruth are well positioned to file a life-changing-event appeal shortly after retiring, providing documentation of their retirement and their new, lower expected income, potentially reducing their Medicare premiums well before the standard lookback would otherwise catch up to their new circumstances on its own. This is a good example of how the concepts in this chapter directly translate into a concrete, actionable step for a very common retirement scenario — leaving full-time work with a meaningful income drop — that many retirees in a similar position never think to take.

How IRMAA Interacts With the Social Security COLA "Hold-Harmless" Provision

A separate protection worth understanding, distinct from the life-changing-event appeal described above, is a provision sometimes referred to as "hold-harmless," which generally applies to Part B premiums specifically (including any IRMAA surcharge, in some interpretations, though the core hold-harmless protection is most directly tied to the standard premium) for beneficiaries who have their premiums deducted directly from their Social Security check. In broad terms, this provision is designed to prevent a beneficiary's net Social Security payment from decreasing year-over-year solely because a Part B premium increase outpaced that year's COLA increase — protecting against the scenario where a premium increase would otherwise more than offset a small COLA adjustment, leaving someone with less net income than the year before.

This hold-harmless protection generally does not apply to everyone in every circumstance — for instance, it generally doesn't protect new enrollees in their first year of Part B coverage, and higher-income beneficiaries already paying IRMAA surcharges are generally not covered by this specific protection for the surcharge portion of their premium. Because the interaction between COLA, standard premium changes, and IRMAA surcharges involves several moving parts that change from year to year, this is a good example of a topic worth asking the SSA about directly if you notice your net Social Security payment changing in a way you don't understand, rather than trying to reconstruct the calculation yourself from general descriptions.

Planning Ahead for IRMAA Before You Retire

Because of the two-year lookback described earlier in this chapter, one of the more valuable planning windows for managing IRMAA is actually before you retire, not after. If you're a few years out from retirement and already have a rough sense of your expected income in your final working years versus your expected income in early retirement, it's worth modeling out — ideally with a financial or tax advisor — how that transition might affect your IRMAA tier in your first year or two on Medicare, and whether proactively filing a life-changing-event appeal immediately upon retiring (as illustrated above with Alden and Ruth) is likely to apply to your situation.

This kind of advance modeling is also the right time to think through the timing of any planned large one-time income events — a Roth conversion, the sale of a business or investment property, or similar — relative to when you expect to enroll in Medicare, since income in a given year can affect IRMAA determinations roughly two years later, meaning decisions made well before your Medicare enrollment date can still ripple into your premiums after you're on Medicare. Working backward from your anticipated Medicare enrollment date, and mapping out your expected income two years prior to that date and beyond, is a more effective way to manage IRMAA proactively than waiting to react to a surprise premium notice after the fact.

IRMAA for Spouses

It's worth clarifying that IRMAA determinations for married couples filing jointly are generally based on the couple's combined MAGI compared against joint-filer thresholds, and each spouse's premium surcharge, if any, is then generally assessed individually based on that same joint income figure and the joint thresholds — meaning one spouse's higher earnings can push both spouses into a higher IRMAA tier, even if the other spouse's individual income would not have triggered a surcharge on its own. This is worth understanding clearly for couples where one spouse has notably higher income than the other, since it means IRMAA planning genuinely needs to consider the household's combined MAGI, not just the income of the spouse actually enrolled in Medicare, if both spouses are contemplating income-affecting decisions like Roth conversions or continued work in the years surrounding Medicare enrollment.

Putting IRMAA in Perspective

After a chapter devoted to a fairly technical topic, it's worth stepping back and putting IRMAA in perspective: it affects a minority of Medicare beneficiaries — specifically those with higher incomes — and even for those it does affect, it represents a premium surcharge, not a benefit reduction or a penalty in the sense the Part B and Part D late-enrollment penalties from Chapter Eight represent. Being subject to IRMAA is, in a real sense, a byproduct of having a stronger income picture in retirement, which is generally a position most people would prefer to be in rather than avoid. The goal of this chapter isn't to help you avoid having income — it's to help you understand the mechanics well enough to avoid paying more than necessary due to the lookback timing mismatch described throughout this chapter, particularly in the first year or two after a major income change like retirement.

How This Chapter Fits With the Rest of Your Medicare Planning

IRMAA is best understood as one layer of a broader Medicare cost picture that also includes the standard premiums, deductibles, and cost-sharing amounts described in Chapter Eight, and the enrollment timing rules that determine whether you're paying any late-enrollment penalties on top of your regular premiums. When you're mapping out your expected Medicare costs in retirement, it's worth building a picture that includes all of these layers together — standard premiums, any IRMAA surcharge based on your projected MAGI, and confirmation that you're enrolled on time to avoid late penalties — rather than treating each one as a separate, disconnected topic. A financial advisor or Medicare counselor can help you build this fuller picture as part of your overall retirement income and healthcare cost planning, ideally well before you actually reach 65.

A Short Glossary of Terms From This Chapter

Given how many acronyms and specific terms this chapter has introduced, it may help to have them gathered in one place for quick future reference. IRMAA refers to the Income-Related Monthly Adjustment Amount, the income-based surcharge on Part B and Part D premiums covered throughout this chapter. MAGI refers to Modified Adjusted Gross Income, the income measure IRMAA is based on. The "two-year lookback" refers to IRMAA generally being calculated using your tax return from two years prior to the current year. A "life-changing event" refers to one of a specific list of qualifying circumstances — including retirement, marriage, divorce, or the death of a spouse — that allows you to request an IRMAA recalculation based on more current income than the standard lookback would otherwise use, generally via Form SSA-44. Keeping these terms straight makes it considerably easier to navigate both this book and any future conversations you have with the SSA or a financial professional about your Medicare premiums.

A Quick Reference for This Chapter's Key Numbers

To close this chapter, its central mechanics are worth restating together. IRMAA is an income-based surcharge on Part B and Part D premiums, generally calculated from your tax return filed two years before the premium year, using tiered income brackets that adjust periodically. If your income has dropped due to a specific qualifying life-changing event — retirement, marriage, divorce, the death of a spouse, among others — you can request a recalculation using more current income, generally through Form SSA-44, rather than waiting for the standard lookback to catch up on its own. And because IRMAA shares its underlying income measure with the tax-planning topics from the previous chapter, large one-time income events are worth timing with both chapters' thresholds in mind simultaneously, not just one or the other in isolation.

A Closing Perspective on Being Proactive

The recurring lesson of this chapter is that Social Security's administrative systems, however well designed, are not built to automatically catch every individual circumstance in real time — the two-year lookback described throughout this chapter is a reasonable, necessary administrative simplification, but it means the system will not proactively notice that your income has dropped since you retired. It's on you, or your advisor, to notice that gap and act on it through the life-changing-event appeal process. This is a pattern worth carrying forward into the rest of your dealings with Social Security and Medicare more broadly: these are generally well-run, rules-based systems, but they are not designed to anticipate every individual's specific timing or circumstances without you actively engaging with them. Being the one to notice when a general rule doesn't quite fit your specific, current situation — and knowing there's usually a process to address that mismatch, as there is here — is a genuinely valuable habit for navigating Social Security and Medicare over the course of your retirement.

Key Takeaways

IRMAA is an income-based surcharge added to Medicare Part B and Part D premiums, generally calculated using your tax return from two years prior — not your current income.

If your income has dropped significantly due to a specific qualifying life-changing event (such as retirement, divorce, or the death of a spouse), you can request that the SSA use more current income data instead of the standard two-year-old figures, generally via Form SSA-44.

Not every income drop qualifies for this appeal — general investment losses, for example, generally do not — so check with the SSA directly if you're uncertain whether your situation qualifies.

Because IRMAA is based on the same MAGI figure affected by tax-planning decisions like Roth conversions and required minimum distributions, coordinate major income-timing decisions with IRMAA thresholds in mind, ideally with professional guidance.

Chapter Ten: The Social Security Fairness Act and Public Sector Workers

For decades, a specific group of retirees — largely public sector workers such as teachers, firefighters, police officers, and certain federal, state, and local government employees — faced a set of rules that reduced or eliminated Social Security benefits they might otherwise have expected, because of pensions they earned from work not covered by Social Security. In January 2025, the Social Security Fairness Act changed this significantly. This chapter explains what changed, who it affects, and what to do if you believe it applies to you.

The Two Provisions That Were Repealed

Before this legislation, two specific provisions shaped how Social Security interacted with certain government pensions.

The Windfall Elimination Provision (WEP) affected people who earned a pension from work not covered by Social Security (common in certain state and local government jobs, and some other public sector positions) while also qualifying for a Social Security retirement or disability benefit based on other work where they did pay into Social Security. WEP generally reduced the Social Security benefit these individuals would otherwise receive, using a modified, less generous version of the standard benefit formula described in Chapter One.

The Government Pension Offset (GPO) affected spousal and survivor benefits specifically, generally reducing the spousal or survivor benefit a person could receive based on their spouse's (or late spouse's) Social Security record, if that person also received a pension from government work not covered by Social Security. In many cases, GPO reduced these spousal or survivor benefits substantially, and for some people, eliminated them entirely.

Both provisions were originally intended to address a specific technical issue: without some adjustment, people who split their careers between Social Security-covered work and non-covered government work could end up with the progressive Social Security formula treating them as if they were low lifetime earners overall (since only part of their earnings history was captured in the Social Security system), producing a benefit disproportionately generous relative to their actual full career earnings. WEP and GPO were designed to correct for that — but critics argued for decades that the correction was often too blunt, penalizing people more than the underlying issue justified, and creating genuine hardship for retirees who had structured their careers around a reasonable expectation of both a pension and at least a partial Social Security benefit.

What the Social Security Fairness Act Did

The Social Security Fairness Act, signed into law in January 2025, repealed both WEP and GPO. This means that, going forward, public sector workers and their spouses or survivors affected by these provisions are generally no longer subject to the reductions they previously faced, and their Social Security benefits — including their own retirement benefits, and spousal or survivor benefits — are generally calculated using the same standard formulas described throughout this book, without the WEP or GPO adjustments.

The law also included retroactive provisions, generally allowing eligible individuals to receive increased benefit amounts (and in some cases retroactive payments covering a period before the law's effective date) reflecting the removal of these provisions. Because the specific retroactive provisions, effective dates, and any administrative rollout details are the kind of specifics that can involve real complexity and potential updates over time, anyone who believes they were affected by WEP or GPO in the past should check directly with the SSA for the current status of their specific case, rather than relying on general summaries like this one for exact dollar figures or precise dates.

Who Should Pay Particular Attention

If you spent any part of your career in a job that did not withhold Social Security payroll taxes — common examples include certain state and local government positions (teaching is a frequently cited example in many, though not all, states, since Social Security coverage for public school teachers varies by state), some federal employees hired under the older Civil Service Retirement System (CSRS) prior to more recent federal employees generally being covered under a system that does include Social Security, and certain other public sector roles — this chapter applies to you directly, even if you also worked in Social Security-covered jobs at other points in your career.

This also applies to spouses and survivors of people in these situations, since GPO's repeal specifically affects spousal and survivor benefits, not just an individual's own retirement benefit based on their own non-covered pension.

What to Do If You Believe This Affects You

If you previously applied for Social Security benefits and were told your benefit was reduced or eliminated due to WEP or GPO, or if you never applied because you assumed WEP or GPO would eliminate any benefit entirely, this is worth revisiting directly with the SSA now. Given the scale of this legislative change, and the fact that many affected individuals may not be aware of it or may not realize it applies to their specific situation, proactively checking your status — even if you were told years ago that you weren't eligible for a benefit, or that your benefit would be minimal — is a reasonable and potentially valuable step.

Because the administrative process for implementing a change of this scale takes time, and because individual circumstances vary considerably, this is an area where patience combined with direct follow-up with the SSA, rather than assumptions in either direction, will serve you best. If you're unsure how to start, the SSA's website and local field offices are the most reliable current sources for the specific steps involved in requesting a recalculation of your benefit under the new rules.

An Illustration

Consider a hypothetical retiree, Yolanda, who spent 22 years as a public school teacher in a state where teaching positions did not pay into Social Security, earning a pension through her state's teacher retirement system. Earlier in her career, and again for several years after retiring from teaching, she also worked in jobs that did pay into Social Security, accumulating enough credits to qualify for a Social Security retirement benefit in her own right. Under the old WEP rules, her Social Security benefit — based on that Social Security-covered work — would have been significantly reduced because of her teacher's pension. Under the repeal, that reduction generally no longer applies, and her Social Security benefit is calculated using the same standard formula available to any other worker with a similar earnings history.

Separately, consider Yolanda's husband, a career Social Security-covered worker. Before the repeal, if Yolanda had wanted to claim a spousal benefit based on his record, GPO would have substantially reduced or eliminated that spousal benefit because of her teacher's pension. Under the repeal, that offset generally no longer applies either, meaning Yolanda may now be eligible for a more substantial spousal benefit based on her husband's record than she would have been able to receive previously.

The History and Rationale Behind WEP and GPO, in More Depth

Understanding why WEP and GPO existed in the first place — even though they've now been repealed — helps explain why this topic generated such sustained debate for decades, and why the repeal was significant enough to warrant its own chapter in this book.

Social Security's benefit formula, described in Chapter One, is intentionally progressive: it replaces a larger percentage of average lifetime earnings for lower earners than for higher earners. This design assumes that someone with a low recorded average across their 35-year earnings history was, in fact, a low earner throughout their working life. But for someone who spent a substantial part of their career in non-covered government work — earning a separate pension through that work, but no Social Security-covered wages during those years — their Social Security earnings record might show a lower average not because they were a low earner overall, but because a meaningful chunk of their actual career wasn't captured in the Social Security system at all. Without some adjustment, the formula's progressive design could end up treating this person as if they were a low lifetime earner, applying the more generous replacement percentage meant for genuinely low earners, even though their total career earnings (Social Security-covered plus pension-covered) were substantially higher.

WEP was designed to address this specific mismatch by applying a modified, less generous version of the formula to the Social Security-covered portion of these individuals' earnings. GPO addressed a related but distinct issue in spousal and survivor benefits, reasoning that a spousal or survivor benefit is meant to support a spouse who was financially dependent on the working spouse — a rationale that GPO's supporters argued didn't apply in the same way to someone who had their own substantial pension from non-covered government work.

Critics of both provisions argued for decades that the adjustments were frequently too blunt — reducing benefits by more than the underlying mismatch actually justified, and creating genuine financial hardship for long-serving public employees and their families who had reasonably planned around receiving both a pension and at least a partial Social Security benefit. This tension between the formula's original progressive design and its unintended effect on mixed-career public employees was the central argument behind the eventual push for repeal.

How to Check If You Were Affected

If you're unsure whether WEP or GPO applied to your own situation historically, a few signals are worth checking. If you receive, or expect to receive, a pension from work where Social Security taxes were not withheld from your paycheck, WEP may have applied to any Social Security retirement benefit you were separately entitled to based on other covered work. If you receive, or expect to receive, that same kind of non-covered pension and you were also eligible for a spousal or survivor benefit based on a spouse's or ex-spouse's Social Security record, GPO may have applied to that spousal or survivor benefit specifically.

If either of these descriptions sounds like it could apply to you, and you haven't already confirmed your current status with the SSA following the Fairness Act repeal, that follow-up is worth prioritizing — both to correct your ongoing benefit amount going forward and to inquire about any retroactive payments you may be entitled to under the law's retroactive provisions.

What This Means for Current and Future Public Sector Workers

For people currently working in non-covered government positions, or considering such a position, the repeal of WEP and GPO changes the financial calculus of mixed-career planning meaningfully. Previously, someone splitting a career between covered and non-covered work needed to factor in the likelihood of a reduced Social Security benefit (and reduced spousal or survivor benefits for a spouse) as a real cost of that career path. With WEP and GPO repealed, Social Security benefits earned through covered work are generally calculated using the same standard formula available to any other worker, regardless of separate pension income from non-covered work, removing a financial disincentive that some critics argued had discouraged qualified people from entering or remaining in certain public service careers, particularly teaching and public safety roles in states where those positions don't participate in Social Security.

It's worth noting that this repeal doesn't change whether a given job is Social Security-covered or not — that's a separate question determined by each state's and employer's participation agreements, unrelated to the

Fairness Act. What changed is how Social Security benefits are calculated for people who do have a non-covered pension, not whether a particular job pays into Social Security in the first place.

A Second Illustration: A Firefighter's Household

Consider a hypothetical retired firefighter, Marcus, who spent 28 years with a municipal fire department in a state where firefighters do not pay into Social Security, earning a solid pension through the fire department's own retirement system. Earlier in his life, before joining the fire department, Marcus worked for several years in private-sector jobs that did pay into Social Security, accumulating just enough credits to qualify for a small Social Security retirement benefit in his own right, though under the old WEP rules, that small benefit would have been further reduced.

Marcus's wife, Denise, worked a full career in Social Security-covered private-sector employment with a substantial earnings record of her own. Under the old GPO rules, if Marcus had ever wanted to claim a spousal benefit based on Denise's record (in a scenario where his own benefit was lower), that spousal benefit would likely have been eliminated entirely because of his firefighter's pension. Under the repeal, both the WEP reduction to Marcus's own small Social Security benefit and the GPO reduction to any potential spousal benefit based on Denise's record generally no longer apply, meaningfully changing the household's Social Security-related income compared to what they would have received under the prior rules.

State-by-State Variation in Which Public Jobs Are Covered

One detail worth understanding clearly is that whether a specific public sector job pays into Social Security at all is determined by decisions made at the state and local level, generally through agreements between individual states and the Social Security Administration dating back several decades, along with more recent decisions by individual public employers. This means the answer to "does my job pay into Social Security" varies considerably not just by profession but by exactly which state, and sometimes which specific school district, municipality, or agency, you work for. A teacher in one state may be fully covered by Social Security through their teaching position, while a teacher in a neighboring state, doing essentially the same job, may not be covered at all and instead relies entirely on a separate state teacher retirement system.

Because of this variation, it's genuinely not possible to state a general rule like "teachers don't pay into Social Security" or "firefighters don't pay into Social Security" as a nationwide fact — it depends entirely on your specific state and employer. If you're unsure whether your own public sector position is Social Security-covered, your pay stub is the most direct way to check: a Social Security-covered position will show Social Security payroll tax withholding (sometimes labeled "OASDI" on a pay stub) alongside any pension contributions, while a non-covered position generally will not show that specific withholding line, even though pension contributions may still be withheld separately.

A Brief, Neutral Note on the Fairness Act's Broader Context

Legislation of this scale inevitably involves policy trade-offs and cost considerations at the federal budget level, which were part of the public debate around the Social Security Fairness Act both before and after its passage. This book intentionally does not take a position on those broader policy debates — its purpose is to help you understand how the current law affects your own eligibility and benefit calculation, not to evaluate the wisdom of the underlying policy choice. If you're interested in the broader fiscal and policy context surrounding this legislation, official government sources, including SSA's own public communications and Congressional Budget Office analyses, are more appropriate and more rigorously sourced places to explore that dimension than a practical planning guide like this one.

Where to Get Help If Your Case Involves Unusual Complexity

Some readers' work histories involve genuinely unusual complexity — multiple periods of non-covered government work interspersed with covered private-sector work, work in more than one state with different coverage rules, or a combination of the topics covered in multiple chapters of this book (for instance, someone with both a non-covered pension and a divorced-spouse benefit claim, combining the topics of this chapter and Chapter Six). If your situation involves this kind of layered complexity, a general guide like this one, however thorough, has real limits in what it can address with confidence.

In these more complex cases, it's worth specifically seeking out an SSA representative or a financial advisor with direct experience handling cases involving non-covered government pensions, rather than a general-practice advisor without that specific background, since the interactions between these provisions can be genuinely intricate and the financial stakes of an error or a missed benefit can be substantial. Local SSA field offices, some of which are located near concentrations of public sector employers, can sometimes offer particularly relevant experience with these situations.

A Note for Readers Currently Weighing a Public Sector Career

If you're earlier in your career and weighing whether to pursue a position in the public sector — including one that might not pay into Social Security — the repeal covered in this chapter removes what was, for decades, a genuine financial complication from that decision. Under the current rules, a mixed career spanning both covered and non-covered work generally no longer carries the same historical risk of a reduced Social Security benefit or reduced spousal and survivor benefits for your family. This doesn't mean

Social Security coverage should be the deciding factor in a career choice that involves many other considerations — compensation, benefits, mission, and personal fit all matter — but it does mean this particular financial concern, which affected many people's career decisions and retirement planning for a long time, carries substantially less weight than it once did.

Verifying Your Own Status Is Worth Repeating

Given how significant this legislative change is, and how many people it affects, it bears repeating one more time as this chapter closes: if any part of your career, or a spouse's or ex-spouse's career, involved non-covered government work, and you have not specifically confirmed your current benefit status with the SSA since the Fairness Act's passage in January 2025, that follow-up remains one of the more valuable, concrete actions available to you from this entire book. Whether the outcome is a corrected ongoing benefit, a retroactive payment, or simply confirmation that your situation was already being handled correctly, the certainty of knowing is worth the relatively modest effort of checking.

A Note for Adult Children of Affected Retirees

If you have a parent or older family member who spent part of their career in public service — teaching, firefighting, law enforcement, or another role that may not have paid into Social Security — this chapter is worth sharing with them directly, or reading together, since many affected retirees are not following retirement-planning publications closely enough to have encountered news of the Fairness Act's passage on their own. Given the scale of the change described in this chapter, and the fact that it can mean a meaningfully larger monthly benefit or a retroactive payment for someone who was told years ago that WEP or GPO eliminated their eligibility, helping an older family member follow up with the SSA on this specific point is one of the more concretely valuable things you can do for them based on the contents of this book.

A Quick Reference for This Chapter's Key Numbers

To close this chapter, its central facts are worth restating together. WEP historically reduced Social Security retirement benefits for people who also received a pension from non-covered government work. GPO historically reduced or eliminated spousal and survivor benefits for people receiving such a pension. Both were repealed by the Social Security Fairness Act, signed into law in January 2025, generally restoring standard benefit calculations going forward, with retroactive provisions covering certain past periods. And whether a specific job is Social Security-covered varies by state and employer, so "teachers don't pay into Social Security" or similar broad statements are never reliably true nationwide — always confirm your own or your family member's specific coverage status directly.

Key Takeaways

The Windfall Elimination Provision (WEP) and Government Pension Offset (GPO) previously reduced or eliminated Social Security benefits for many public sector workers with pensions from non-covered work, and for their spouses and survivors.

The Social Security Fairness Act, signed into law in January 2025, repealed both provisions, generally restoring standard benefit calculations for affected individuals, with retroactive provisions covering certain past periods.

This change affects teachers and other public employees in states where those jobs don't pay into Social Security, certain federal employees under older pension systems, and the spouses and survivors of all of these groups.

If you were previously told your benefit was reduced or eliminated due to WEP or GPO, or assumed you weren't eligible for that reason, check directly with the SSA now — the scale of this change means many eligible people may not yet be aware it applies to them.

Chapter Eleven: Building Your Personal Claiming Strategy

You've now covered the core mechanics: how benefits are calculated, how claiming age affects your monthly amount, how spousal and survivor and divorced-spouse benefits work, how taxation and Medicare and IRMAA fit into the picture, and how the Fairness Act changed things for many public sector workers. This final chapter is about pulling those pieces together into a practical, personal process — not a generic answer, but a structured way of thinking through your own situation.

Step One: Get Your Real Numbers

Everything before this point in the book has been general. Your actual decision-making needs to start with your specific numbers. Create or log into your "my Social Security" account at ssa.gov and pull your personalized benefit estimates at different claiming ages. If you're married or divorced from a marriage lasting 10+ years, consider what you know about your spouse's or ex-spouse's earnings record as well, since their record may factor into your own household's optimal strategy, as discussed in Chapters Four through Six.

If you believe WEP or GPO may have affected you or a family member in the past, as discussed in Chapter Ten, this is also the moment to follow up directly with the SSA about your current status under the Fairness Act repeal.

Step Two: Map Your Household's Full Income Picture

Social Security is rarely the entire retirement income picture. List out every other source of retirement income available to your household: pensions, retirement account balances and expected withdrawal patterns, any part-time work income you anticipate, and other savings or investments. Understanding how much of your retirement expenses these other sources can cover on their own — independent of when you claim Social Security — will clarify how much flexibility you actually have in your claiming-age decision. A household that can comfortably cover its expenses from other sources for several years has real flexibility to delay claiming; a household without that cushion may have a more constrained, though still legitimate, set of choices.

Step Three: Think Through Health and Longevity Honestly

This is an uncomfortable step for many people, but an honest, private conversation with yourself (and your spouse, if applicable) about health history and family longevity patterns is a legitimate input into this decision — not a morbid distraction from it. You are not predicting your exact lifespan; you are simply weighing whether your own health picture leans toward "claiming earlier makes practical sense for me" or "the insurance value of waiting is likely to pay off for me," recognizing that neither instinct is guaranteed to be right, because nobody can know this in advance with certainty.

Step Four: Weigh the Household Dimension, Not Just Your Own

If you are married, revisit Chapters Four and Five specifically. Ask: whose earnings record is higher? What would our household's income look like if the higher earner passed away first, under different claiming-age scenarios for that higher earner? Because the higher earner's claiming decision sets the ceiling for the eventual survivor benefit, this question often reframes what initially looks like an individual decision into a household-protection decision — and for many couples, this single consideration shifts the "right" answer meaningfully compared to looking at either spouse's numbers in isolation.

If you are divorced from a marriage that lasted 10 years or more, revisit Chapter Six and make sure you've checked your eligibility for divorced-spouse or divorced-survivor benefits, since these are commonly overlooked entirely.

Step Five: Factor In Taxes and Medicare Timing

Pull in the concepts from Chapters Seven, Eight, and Nine. Consider how your claiming decision interacts with your broader tax picture — combined income thresholds, required minimum distributions, and any Roth conversion strategy you might be considering. Separately, and regardless of when you decide to claim Social Security, mark your Medicare Initial Enrollment Period on a calendar well before you turn 65, and confirm whether you qualify for an employer-coverage exception or need to actively enroll during that window. These two systems run on their own timelines, and treating them as a single combined decision (rather than two related but separate ones) is one of the most common sources of costly, avoidable mistakes.

Step Six: Talk to a Professional Before You File

Nothing in this book is a substitute for sitting down with the SSA directly, or with a financial advisor or tax professional who can see your complete financial picture, before you actually submit a claiming application. The concepts in this book are meant to prepare you for that conversation — to help you ask sharper questions, understand the answers you're given, and recognize when something being explained to you doesn't sound quite right — not to replace that conversation entirely.

A useful frame: think of this book as preparing you to be a well-informed participant in your own financial decisions, not as a replacement for the professionals and official resources who can see your actual numbers and confirm the current rules.

A Simple Framework to Carry Forward

If you take only one structural habit from this entire book, let it be this: before making any Social Security or Medicare decision, ask three questions. What does this decision look like for me individually? What does it look like for my household, including a surviving spouse if applicable? And what does it look like once taxes, Medicare timing, and any income-related surcharges are factored in? Most costly mistakes in this space come from answering only the first question and treating it as the whole answer.

Revisiting This Book Over Time

Because Social Security and Medicare rules, thresholds, and figures are periodically updated, and because your own circumstances will continue to evolve as you approach and move through retirement, consider this book something to return to rather than something to read once and set aside. The mechanics described here — how the formulas work, how the different benefit categories relate to each other, how the enrollment windows function — tend to remain stable even as the specific dollar figures and thresholds around them are periodically adjusted. Revisiting the relevant chapter when you're facing a specific decision, with current figures pulled fresh from ssa.gov or medicare.gov, is a sound way to use this book throughout your retirement planning process, not just once at the outset.

A Simple Worksheet You Can Use

To turn the six steps above into something concrete, consider working through the following questions on paper, ideally with your spouse if applicable, before your first serious conversation with the SSA or a financial advisor.

What is my own estimated benefit at 62, at my FRA, and at 70, according to my "my Social Security" account? If married or divorced from a 10-plus-year marriage, what is my spouse's or ex-spouse's estimated benefit at those same three ages, to the extent I know or can reasonably estimate it? What other income sources will my household have in retirement, and roughly when do they begin? How comfortable am I, honestly, with my own or my household's health outlook and family longevity patterns? If I'm married, what would my household's income look like if the higher earner passed away first, under a few different claiming-age scenarios for that higher earner? Do I have any history of non-covered government work, or does my spouse, that might connect to the topics in Chapter Ten? When do I turn 65, and have I mapped out my Medicare enrollment plan separately from my Social Security claiming plan? Roughly what will my combined income look like in the first few years of retirement, and does that suggest any of my Social Security benefit is likely to be taxable?

Working through these questions doesn't require having a final answer to all of them before you talk to a professional — in fact, bringing an incomplete worksheet with clear, specific questions to that conversation is often more productive than trying to resolve everything on your own first.

Common Regrets Retirees Report

Surveys and anecdotal reports from retirees fairly consistently surface a few recurring regrets related to Social Security decisions, and it's worth naming them here as a final, practical caution. Claiming earlier than necessary out of anxiety about the program's long-term funding, rather than because of an actual, considered need for the income, is a commonly cited regret among people who later found they had other resources that could have supported a longer delay. Not fully understanding spousal or survivor benefit implications until after a claiming decision was already locked in is another frequently cited regret, particularly among people who claimed individually without fully thinking through the household perspective discussed throughout this book. And missing a Medicare enrollment window, resulting in a permanent late-enrollment penalty that could have been avoided with a bit more advance planning, is a third common and entirely avoidable regret.

None of these regrets reflect a lack of intelligence or effort on the part of the people who experienced them — they largely reflect how genuinely confusing and interconnected this system is, which is precisely the gap this book has aimed to close.

When to Revisit Your Strategy After You've Filed

Even after you've claimed Social Security and enrolled in Medicare, it's worth periodically revisiting a few things. If your income changes significantly — through continued part-time work, a change in investment income, or a change in marital status — revisit Chapter Seven's tax implications and Chapter Nine's IRMAA implications, since your ongoing situation may shift even after your initial claiming decision is locked in. If you experience a qualifying life-changing event as described in Chapter Nine, don't assume your Medicare premiums will automatically adjust — file the appropriate paperwork proactively. And if new legislation affecting Social Security or Medicare is enacted — as the Social Security Fairness Act was in January 2025 — it's worth checking whether it affects your specific situation, even years after you've already filed, rather than assuming that decisions made under old rules are permanently fixed regardless of legal changes.

A Final Practical Checklist

As you move from reading this book to taking action, consider working through this short checklist: create or log into your "my Social Security" account and review your estimated benefits at multiple ages; review your earnings record for accuracy; if applicable, gather documentation related to a current or former spouse's record; map your full household income picture across all sources, not just Social Security; mark your Medicare Initial Enrollment Period on a calendar well before you turn 65; consider your tax withholding strategy for Social Security benefits once you begin claiming; and schedule time with the SSA directly, and with a financial or tax advisor if you work with one, before you submit any formal claiming application. Each of these steps is manageable on its own, and together they form a solid foundation for approaching this decision with clarity rather than guesswork.

Building a Support Team

Rather than thinking of this as a decision you need to make entirely on your own, it may help to think of it as a decision supported by a small team, each member handling a different piece. The Social Security Administration itself is the authoritative source for your specific benefit estimates, eligibility questions, and application process — free of charge, and worth using directly rather than only through secondhand summaries. A financial advisor, if you work with one, can help model your claiming-age decision against your full household financial picture, including the household and survivor-benefit dimensions covered throughout this book. A tax professional can help you navigate the taxation topics from Chapter Seven and the IRMAA topics from Chapter Nine, particularly around the timing of retirement account withdrawals and any large one-time income events. And for Medicare specifically, a Medicare counselor — including free, unbiased counseling available through many state programs, sometimes called SHIP (State Health Insurance Assistance Program) counseling — can help you navigate the Part B, Part D, Medicare Advantage, and Medigap decisions from Chapter Eight without the potential bias of a plan-specific sales conversation.

You don't need all of these resources simultaneously, and not everyone will need every one of them — but knowing they exist, and roughly which topics each one is best suited to help with, makes it easier to seek out the right kind of help at the right time rather than either avoiding the decision entirely or trying to become an expert in every domain covered by this book yourself.

A Sample Timeline From Age 60 to 67

To make the multi-year nature of this planning process concrete, consider a general timeline many readers might follow, adjusted to your own specific ages and FRA. Around age 60, if applicable, begin exploring survivor benefit eligibility if you've lost a spouse, since survivor benefits can begin at this age, as covered in Chapter Five. Around age 60 to 62, create your "my Social Security" account if you haven't already, and begin reviewing your personalized benefit estimates at different claiming ages, along with your earnings record for accuracy. Around age 62, if you're considering claiming at the earliest eligible age, revisit Chapters Two and Three carefully, and if married, revisit Chapters Four and Five with your spouse before finalizing a decision. In the two to three years before you turn 65, begin researching your Medicare enrollment plan specifically, following Chapter Eight, independent of whatever your Social Security claiming timeline looks like. Around age 65, actively enroll in Medicare during your Initial Enrollment Period unless you have a qualifying employer-coverage exception, and if you're retiring around this time, consider whether the IRMAA life-changing-event appeal from Chapter Nine applies to your situation. Between your FRA and age 70, if you're delaying your Social Security claim, periodically revisit your household's income needs and reconsider whether continuing to delay still makes sense given how your circumstances have evolved. And at age 70, if you haven't already claimed, file your Social Security application, since there's no further financial benefit to delaying past this age, as covered in Chapter Two.

This timeline is illustrative, not prescriptive — your own path may look quite different depending on your FRA, your health, your household situation, and your specific circumstances covered throughout this book. Its purpose is simply to show that this is a years-long process with natural checkpoints, not a single decision made in isolation on one particular day.

Final Thoughts on Confidence Over Perfection

It's worth closing this chapter with a reminder that the goal of everything covered in this book is not to help you find some theoretically perfect, mathematically optimal claiming strategy — a goal that isn't fully achievable anyway, since it depends on unknowable future variables like your own lifespan and future changes to tax law. The more realistic and genuinely achievable goal is a well-informed, deliberate decision that fits your household's actual circumstances, made with a clear understanding of the trade-offs involved, rather than a decision made by default, out of anxiety, or without understanding the mechanics well enough to ask the right questions.

If you finish this book with a clearer sense of the questions to ask, the resources to consult, and the interconnections between claiming age, spousal and survivor benefits, taxation, and Medicare timing — even without a single final number in hand yet — you are in a substantially stronger position than someone approaching this decision without that foundation. That clarity, more than any specific claiming age, is the real objective of this book.

If You're Helping a Parent or Family Member With This Decision

Many readers of this book are not approaching their own claiming decision at all, but are helping an aging parent or other family member navigate theirs. If that describes you, everything covered in this book still applies, with one additional layer worth naming directly: these are your family member's decisions to make, even when you're the one doing the research and organizing the paperwork. Involve them in the process as fully as their capacity allows, explain the trade-offs in the plain terms this book has aimed for rather than jargon, and be mindful that a decision that seems mathematically obvious to you from the outside may carry emotional or values-based weight for them that isn't captured in a spreadsheet. If you do end up serving in a more formal capacity — such as holding power of attorney or acting as a representative payee — the SSA has specific procedures for that role, which are worth understanding directly from the SSA rather than assuming general power-of-attorney documents automatically extend to Social Security matters in every respect.

Closing

You've now worked through the full arc of this book: how benefits are calculated, the claiming-age trade-off and the insurance logic behind it, how spousal, survivor, and divorced-spouse benefits extend and interact with an individual's own benefit, how taxation and IRMAA affect what actually reaches your bank account, how Medicare's separate timeline needs its own attention, and how the Social Security Fairness Act reshaped the picture for a significant group of public sector workers and their families. Each of these pieces connects to the others more than a first glance suggests, which is exactly why a single, integrated understanding — rather than isolated facts about any one piece — is what allows you to make a genuinely well-informed decision. Take that understanding, gather your specific numbers, and take the next concrete step, whether that's creating your ssa.gov account, scheduling time with an advisor, or simply having a focused conversation with your spouse about what you've learned. The decision is yours to make, and you are now considerably better equipped to make it.

One Last Reminder on Verifying Current Figures

As this book closes, it's worth restating its opening caution one final time, because it matters more here than almost anywhere else: every specific number, threshold, percentage, and dollar figure referenced anywhere in this book is a general description of how the underlying mechanism works, not a value to rely on for an actual filing decision. Benefit formulas, tax thresholds, IRMAA brackets, and Medicare premiums are all subject to periodic adjustment, and the specific figures that apply to your actual claim will be the ones in effect at the time you file, verified through ssa.gov, medicare.gov, or a licensed professional — not the general patterns described in a book meant to explain how the system works rather than to serve as a lookup table for current figures. Carrying that habit of verification forward, chapter by chapter and decision by decision, is the single most practical takeaway this book can offer.

A Final Summary Across All Eleven Chapters

As a last, consolidated reference before you move into action, it may help to see the entire arc of this book compressed into a single set of reminders. Your benefit is built from your highest 35 years of covered earnings, run through a formula anchored to your Full Retirement Age, with claiming anywhere from 62 to 70 permanently adjusting that amount up or down. If married, your spousal benefit tops out at 50% of your spouse's PIA, while your eventual survivor benefit can reach up to 100% of what your spouse was receiving — making the higher earner's claiming age a household decision, not just a personal one. If divorced from a marriage lasting 10 years or more, you may hold parallel rights to a former spouse's record, independent of their own filing status and without affecting what they receive. Taxation of your benefits depends on combined income measured against thresholds that vary by filing status and haven't kept pace with inflation, while Medicare enrollment runs on its own strict, largely unforgiving timeline that has nothing to do with your Social Security claiming date. IRMAA can add income-based surcharges to your Medicare premiums, calculated with a two-year lookback that a life-changing-event appeal can correct when your circumstances shift. And if your career, or a family member's, touched public sector work that didn't pay into Social Security, the 2025 Fairness Act likely changed what you're entitled to, in ways worth confirming directly with the SSA if you haven't already.

None of these mechanics require you to become a technical expert in Social Security law. They require you to know enough to ask sharp questions, gather your own real numbers, and involve the right SSA representative or professional at the right moment. That is precisely the foundation this book has aimed to give you, and it's a foundation you can now carry forward into whatever stage of this decision you're currently facing — whether that's years away, right at the threshold, or already underway.

Key Takeaways

Building a personal strategy starts with your real numbers from ssa.gov, not general estimates, and extends to a full household income picture, honest health and longevity considerations, and the household-level implications of spousal and survivor benefits.

Tax planning and Medicare enrollment timing are separate but related systems that deserve their own deliberate attention alongside the core claiming-age decision, not an afterthought handled at the last minute.

This book is preparation for a conversation with the SSA and qualified professionals, not a replacement for it — use it to ask better questions and understand the answers, then confirm your specific numbers and rules before filing.

Because rules and figures change over time, treat this book as a reference to revisit at each new decision point in your retirement journey, not a one-time read.

A Final Word

If there is a single thread running through every chapter of this book, it's this: Social Security and Medicare are more flexible, and more interconnected with the rest of your financial life, than most people realize going in. The claiming-age decision is not just about your own monthly check — it ripples into your spouse's eventual survivor benefit, your tax bracket in retirement, your Medicare premiums, and in some cases, benefits from a marriage that ended years or decades ago.

None of that complexity is meant to be intimidating. It's meant to be navigable, one decision at a time, with the right information in hand. You don't need to become an expert in every provision covered in this book to make a sound decision for your own household — you need to understand the shape of the major trade-offs well enough to ask good questions, gather your specific numbers, and work with the SSA or a qualified professional to fill in the details that apply to your exact situation.

Wherever you are in your own timeline — years away from claiming, right at the decision point, or already receiving benefits and wondering whether you left something on the table — the same basic approach holds: get your real numbers, look at the decision from a household perspective, factor in taxes and Medicare timing, and check in with the SSA directly whenever something in your specific situation doesn't quite match a general description like the ones in this book.

Retirement planning is rarely about finding one perfect, universal answer. It's about making a series of informed, deliberate choices that fit your actual circumstances — and revisiting those choices as your circumstances, and the rules themselves, continue to evolve. I hope this book has given you a clearer, steadier foundation for making those choices with confidence.

About the Author

Preston Wade writes about retirement planning topics with a focus on making complex government programs understandable to everyday readers. Drawing on years spent researching how Social Security, Medicare, and related retirement systems actually work in practice, Preston aims to translate dense program rules into clear, practical guidance that helps readers approach their own retirement decisions with confidence rather than confusion. This is Preston's contribution to a series of straightforward guides written for people who want to understand their options before they sit down with a financial professional or the Social Security Administration itself.

www.ingramcontent.com/pod-product-compliance
Lightning Source LLC
LaVergne TN
LVHW050818061126
851857LV00012B/870
* 9 7 8 4 5 3 3 8 7 4 7 0 3 *